1941

MONTH	WESTERN FRONT	EASTERN FRONT	MEDITERRANEAN	PACIFIC
January			**22:** Italian garrison at Tobruk surrenders	
February			**14:** Afrika Korps lands in Africa	
March	**8:** US Senate passes Lend-Lease Bill		**28:** British defeat Italians at Battle of Cape Matapan	
April			**6:** Germany invades Yugoslavia and declares war on Greece **26:** German tanks enter Athens	
May	**10:** Rudolf Hess parachutes into Scotland **27:** British navy sinks *Bismarck*			
June		**21:** Operation Barbarossa begins	**1:** Germans take Crete	
August	**9:** Churchill and Roosevelt meet in Newfoundland			
September	**23:** General de Gaulle sets up *Comité National Français*	**7:** Siege of Leningrad begins		
November		**3:** German forces take Kursk **7:** Lend-Lease Act extended to USSR **10:** Germans occupy Yalta	**18:** Operation Crusader launched against Italians and Germans in Libya	**14:** US orders evacuation of troops from Shanghai, Peking, and Tienstsin **30:** Japanese fleet reported to be moving south from Borneo
December		**5:** Germans defeated outside Moscow	**1:** Rommel besieges Tobruk **11:** Mussolini and Hitler declare war on US	**7:** Japanese attack on Pearl Harbor **8:** US and Britain declare war on Japan

1942

MONTH	WESTERN FRONT	EASTERN FRONT	MEDITERRANEAN	PACIFIC
January	**1:** Representatives of 26 nations sign the Atlantic Charter	**18:** Red Army begins advance from Kharkov	**17:** Axis forces of Sollum and Halaya surrender **18:** Rommel begins counterattack	**10:** British abandon Port Swettenham and Kuala Lumpur; Japanese land on Borneo
February	**1:** Puppet government under Quisling established in Norway	**26:** German 16th Army suffers at Satray Russa		**1:** US task forces launch attacks on Japanese bases in Marshall Islands and Gilbert Islands **27:** Japanese victory in naval Battle of Java Sea
March				**7:** Java falls to Japanese **8:** Japanese enter Rangoon **22:** Japanese air raids on Darwin, Australia
April				**18:** First US air raid on Japan
May			**26:** Rommel res... offensive in West... Desert	

D1412493

WORLD WAR II
COLLECTIBLES

An A2 flying jacket, worn by a US pilot, stationed at Duxford in Britain. The small winged foot on the left hand pocket denotes the fact that the pilot was shot down in enemy territory but managed to evade capture and return.

WORLD WAR II
COLLECTIBLES

THE COLLECTOR'S GUIDE TO SELECTING AND CONSERVING
WARTIME MEMORABILIA

Harry Rinker Jr. and Robert Heistand

COURAGE
BOOKS
AN IMPRINT OF
RUNNING PRESS
PHILADELPHIA, PENNSYLVANIA

A QUINTET BOOK

Canadian Representatives:
General Publishing Co., Ltd.
30 Lesmill Road, Don Mills
Ontario M3B 2T6

9 8 7 6 5 4 3 2 1
Digit on the right indicates the number of this printing

Library of Congress
Cataloging-in-Publication Number
92-54942

ISBN 1-56138-217-5

This book was designed and produced by
Quintet Publishing Limited
6 Blundell Street
London N7 9BH

Creative Director: Richard Dewing
Designer: Ian Hunt
Project Editor: Damian Thompson
Editor: Lydia Darbyshire
Photographers: Harry Rinker Jnr.,
Paul Forrester and Martin Norris

Photographs on the following pages reproduced
by kind permission of the Trustees of the
Imperial War Museum:
title page; 7; 13 below; 17; 23; 33 left; 42 above and
below; 44 below; 45; 46; 51 right; 54 above; 56 above
right; 58 above; 61; 62 below; 63 above left; 64 below;
65 left; 66 below; 68 below; 71 above left, below left
and right; 72; 73 below left and right;
74 above right; 76.

Typeset in Great Britain by
Central Southern Typesetters, Eastbourne
Manufactured in Singapore by
Colour Trend
Printed in Singapore by
Star Standard Pte. Ltd.

First published by Courage Books
an imprint of Running Press Book Publishers
125 South Twenty-second Street
Philadelphia, Pennsylvania 19103–4399

CONTENTS

INTRODUCTION

World War I, the war to end all wars, failed to achieve its objective. The Treaty of Versailles, which was signed in June 1919, was agreed to under protest, and it produced only a fragile peace. Its provisions – including restrictions on the size of Germany's army and navy, and the requirement for Germany to pay war reparations – were circumvented and ultimately rejected by Hitler. The resentment felt in Germany combined with a worldwide economic depression during the 1930s and with the increasing influence of Japan in the Far East to exacerbate matters. By the mid-1930s many observers were beginning to regard another European war as inevitable and another world war as likely.

The war that began in Europe in 1939, and that in 1941 spread into the Soviet Union and involved Japan and the United States, led to the mobilization of an estimated 92 million men and women, and caused the deaths of between 35 and 60 million people. Now that more than half a century has passed, however, the collecting of articles associated with the conflict has become increasingly widespread, and more and more people are gathering collections of memorabilia and artifacts that reflect one or more aspects of the war.

Most collectors concentrate on uniforms, equipment, and the personal gear or kit of the combat soldier. Few collectors focus on individual battles, although some specialize in particular theaters of operation. Nevertheless, collectors do discuss key battles and know which units fought in particular campaigns, and they derive satisfaction from being able to link the items they have acquired with specific places and times.

Although the combat soldier remains the primary focus of many collectors' interest, there has been an increase in the attention paid to support units, especially those formed by women, and in items related to the home front.

World War II collectibles are still relatively affordable, even though prices are now measured in hundreds rather than tens of dollars. Prices began to rise appreciably in the 1980s, and this trend shows no signs of abating. Nevertheless, this remains an area in which a collector can acquire a worthwhile and interesting collection for a comparatively moderate outlay.

One of the main difficulties facing today's collectors of objects and memorabilia from World War II is personal prejudice. The war and its aftermath are still sufficiently recent for potential collectors, even if they were not themselves personally involved, to be related to members of the armed forces who took part in the war or, at the very least, to have friends and acquaintances whose own families were directly affected in one way or another. The views of many collectors have been shaped by television and the cinema, even though few of the movies made in the late 1940s or in the 1950s gave wholly accurate views of the war. It is only comparatively recently that the media have offered more realistic portrayals of the horrors endured by soldiers and civilians alike. In addition, each collector brings a different perspective to bear on the subject: the Italians view the war quite differently from, say, the French; and the Russians, British, Germans, Japanese, and Americans all regard the war in different ways. Ask an American when the war began, and he will say 1941. The answer is very different for a Pole or a Belgian.

The growing interest in collecting and preserving articles from World War II is given added impetus by the fact that as the people who survived the war die, the objects they acquired may well be lost. As important as the loss of the items themselves is the lost opportunity to document and record the source and post-war history of the objects. Until recently collectors did not place a great deal of emphasis on provenance, but this is changing as it is realized that a well-documented provenance can enhance both the significance and value of an item.

Another reason for collecting material from this period is the fact that the war marked a clear watershed in the history of the world. Life in the 1930s was very different from life in the 1950s. The social and technological changes that had taken place during the war laid the foundations for the present, and collections of World War II memorabilia are one of the ways in which we can see more clearly and understand more completely the ways in which our own society functions.

LEFT **A dancing cut-out figure depicting Hitler on the front and his skeleton on the reverse side.**

UNIFORMS

CHAPTER I

Combat uniforms are those uniforms that have been designed for the specific purpose of combat. In Britain they are known appropriately as battledress.

Troops often initially entered combat zones wearing regulation dress, but the ravages of fighting were hard on uniforms. Replacement supplies from behind the lines were not always forthcoming, and soldiers tended to take what was available and to "make do." Veteran combat soldiers, therefore, often wore odd mixtures of original issue, items from other friendly troops or occasionally fallen foes, and even articles that were stolen or borrowed on the spot.

The problem of building up a collection of these uniforms is further complicated by the fact that most countries redesigned their combat uniforms as the war progressed, and it is not uncommon to find several different issues in the same theater of operations. Similarly, shortages of supplies and of raw materials necessitated that changes be made by the manufacturers. The collector has, therefore, an almost limitless variety from which to choose.

The distinction between combat uniform and military dress uniform must be noted. Military dress uniform was issued for use on ceremonial occasions – changes of command, formal functions, and parades, for example – and in special areas such as rear-echelon headquarters and in other locations where a smart appearance was warranted. The military dress uniform is not the same as the formal dress uniform, which was worn primarily by officers attending important public functions, and it was not worn in combat zones. The military dress uniform, on the other hand, was worn by military personnel as they traveled on leave or on pass. It might be defined as an informal formal uniform. Combat soldiers did not take military dress uniforms into combat. These uniforms were kept at the soldiers' last garrison before entering the combat zone.

BRITAIN AND THE
·········· COMMONWEALTH ············

British enlisted military personnel used the same basic uniform for dress and combat purposes because of shortages in supplies and the need to conserve materials. When military dress uniform was required, ribbons and distinctive headgear were added to the combat uniform. Commonwealth troops also followed this practice.

This use of one basic uniform to serve two purposes meant that British and Commonwealth soldiers looked smart even under the most trying circumstances. Other nations, noticing this, modified their own uniforms accordingly, and the British combination military dress/combat uniform influenced military dress fashion for three decades.

COMBAT UNIFORMS In common with most European nations involved in World War II, Britain retained the basic uniform that had seen duty in World War I. During the economically depressed years of the late 1920s and 1930s, the government had cut back on military spending, with design and development continuing at only a modest level. It was during this period that the new Pattern (19)37 battledress uniform was designed, a uniform that set a trend in military fashion that is still seen among the combat forces of many nations.

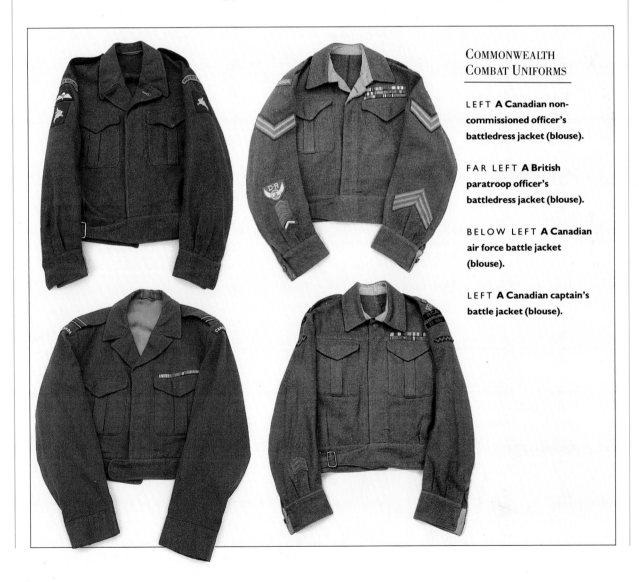

COMMONWEALTH COMBAT UNIFORMS

LEFT **A Canadian non-commissioned officer's battledress jacket (blouse).**

FAR LEFT **A British paratroop officer's battledress jacket (blouse).**

BELOW LEFT **A Canadian air force battle jacket (blouse).**

LEFT **A Canadian captain's battle jacket (blouse).**

The Pattern 37 short battle jacket (blouse) was made of wool. It featured exposed pockets and frontal buttons. A later version with concealed buttons proved to be more popular, and it was used by all nations except Australia, which preferred the exposed-button version.

The Canadians quickly adopted the Pattern 37 combat uniform, which was issued in large quantities to Canadian as well as to other Commonwealth troops. The uniform looked smart, even though it was designed for field use, and because the Canadian battle jackets (blouses) were superior in both material and manufacture, they were eagerly sought after by British officers. The Canadian-manufactured uniforms had concealed buttons, and they tended to be more green than brown when compared with the other Commonwealth- and British-made uniforms. Canadian insignia and rank insignia were similar to those of the British territorial regiments. Kilts continued to be issued to Highland regiments, although the khaki field combat uniform was more often worn.

During the war an attempt was made to standardize battledress, although the material used varied according to the climate and theater of operation. Khaki battle jackets (blouses) were issued to troops in desert or dry areas, and olive-drab jackets (blouses) were worn by troops elsewhere.

ABOVE **New Zealand wool tropical shorts.**

The lime green jungle uniform is difficult to find since few survived the tough conditions in which it saw service, and it was, in any case, issued in only limited quantities.

MILITARY DRESS UNIFORMS The military dress uniform worn by officers featured the traditional four-pocket jacket (blouse), which was complemented with either a cloth belt or a Sam Browne belt. Many officers wore the jacket (blouse) only when decorum required, otherwise appearing in shirt and tie. Officers who served in the tropics had a khaki uniform that was identical to the one worn in Europe.

The trouser pattern was much the same for British and Commonwealth troops. Variations can be found in color, buttons, and the quality of the wool used, and in most cases the country of manufacture may be identified by the type of buttons used.

During the first years of the war, tropical units dressed informally, and little emphasis was placed on regulation battledress and uniformity. Eventually, however, most British and Commonwealth forces adopted a khaki tropical dress consisting of shirt and shorts. The bush jacket (blouse), a popular carry-over from colonial forces, was widely worn in many theaters.

British footwear remained virtually unchanged from the styles used in World War I. Initially, most infantrymen were issued with low boots with puttees (long strips of cloth wound spirally round the leg from ankle to knee). Puttees were replaced by low gaiters during the war, although some colonial forces in India and Europe continued to wear puttees to the very end. Some officers used the double-buckle style boot that was issued to US forces, but this was not a regular occurrence. Riding boots continued to be worn by many staff officers, but they seem to have been rare among field and company grade officers. Officers' dress uniform footwear depended on whether the officer was in a cavalry or infantry regiment. Cavalry officers wore brown riding boots: infantry officers wore brown oxfords (low shoes, lacing over the instep). Breeches or trousers were worn accordingly.

The swagger stick, the stick carried by British officers and warrant officers on duty as an insignia of command, was made of wood or, if the officer were serving in the tropics, of bamboo. Some swagger sticks are polished wood; others are covered in leather. All display the regimental badge embossed on the silver knob.

The military dress uniform was an important part of the ethos of the officers' mess, a tradition that British officers maintained throughout the war whenever circumstances permitted. Their persistence in upholding the practice did much to contribute to sustaining the morale of the British forces.

The military dress uniform of Commonwealth troops was identical to that of the British army. The insignia, ribbons, crests, and other badges are the only means of telling one from the other. Collectors should, therefore, endeavour always to obtain the provenance of any British military dress uniform that they purchase, and, ideally, this record should be kept with the uniform as it is passed from collector to collector.

DRESS UNIFORMS

LEFT **A British artillery captain's tropical dress jacket (blouse).**

RIGHT **The dress jacket (blouse) of an officer in the British Army Medical Corps.**

LEFT **A Canadian officer's shirt, tie and jacket (blouse).**

RIGHT **The dress overcoat of a non-commissioned officer in a Canadian artillery regiment.**

OTHER FORCES EQUIPPED WITH ···BRITISH COMBAT UNIFORMS···

BELGIUM Belgium, which received British support before and during the war, supplied a limited number of troops to the Allied forces. The Belgian pre-war uniforms were exactly the same as British uniforms except for the insignia and distinctive headgear. After Belgium fell to the Germans in May 1940, Belgian troops that escaped were re-equipped with British kit and uniforms. Insignia and distinctive headgear were retained to maintain the Belgian *esprit de corps.*

NORWAY The Germans invaded Norway in April 1940, and a combined Allied force attempt to retake the country failed. The Norwegian forces that managed to withdraw with the Allies were in poor shape, and their original equipment was ill suited to modern warfare. The small Norwegian contingent was outfitted with standard British equipment, although, like the Belgians, they kept their distinctive insignia.

POLAND Poland deserves special attention since it was the first nation to experience the military might of the Third Reich. The Polish forces were ill equipped and out maneuvred, but their willingness to fight showed the unquenchable courage of the nation. Large numbers of Polish forces, fiercely determined to continue the fight, managed to escape to Britain, and Polish forces within the British combined military forces were equipped with British Pattern 37 uniforms. Even the headgear followed the British pattern. Distinctive national insignia and rank insignia were worn when available, although they were frequently not used, partly because of their scarcity, and partly because they caused confusion about the Polish ranks within the Allied forces. All Polish military personnel included the Poland tab on the shoulders of their battle jackets (blouses).

··················· FRANCE ···················

In 1939 France was using the same basic uniform pattern with which it had ended World War I, although the color had changed from horizon blue to olive-drab. In many reserve units, bits and pieces of the horizon blue uniform still appeared, more commonly among officers than enlisted men. Legionnaires wore mostly British uniforms, with a few remnants of the French uniform being retained throughout the war.

After the fall of North Africa, both the military dress and combat uniforms of the Free French forces were supplied by the Americans, and they were distinguished from their American counterparts only by the insignia and headgear, although many Free French troops wore the US M1 style helmet. These uniforms were the standard-issue 1941 combat uniform, consisting of olive-drab wool shirt, khaki wool field scarf, olive green wool web belt with buckle, brown leather field boots, and khaki leggings. Large number of M1941 field jackets (blouses) were issued to the Free French troops. Armored personnel received lined tanker jackets (blouses) with knitted cuffs. Most overcoats were the standard melton (a heavy wool fabric, with a smooth surface and short nap), with plain plastic buttons instead of brass or plastic US eagle buttons.

··················· GERMANY ···················

COMBAT UNIFORMS Few changes were made to the combat uniforms and equipment of the German armed forces until 1936 because of the restrictions placed on Germany by the Treaty of Versailles. The first major change to a uniform occurred when Hitler rapidly expanded the Wehrmacht.

The combat uniform retained the same field gray color as the older pattern. The jacket (blouse) had a stand and fall collar, with pebble-finish buttons on the front, and epaulettes. Cuffs were the French turn-back style.

Officers' rank insignia were worn on the shoulder boards, while non-commissioned officers wore their rank insignia on their left sleeves. Shoulder boards and collar tabs had edge piping in a variety of colors to denote the various branches of service. Tunic pockets were scalloped and pleated. Before 1942 uniforms were made of excellent quality wool.

German uniforms underwent a number of changes during the war as shortages of raw materials forced the military to economize. Changes were also made necessary by the increasing diversity of climate and terrain in which the troops fought and by the variety of tactical requirements to which they were subjected.

In the middle of the war the desire to speed production and conserve materials led to the development of a no-frills tunic. Gone were the French cuffs, dark green collar, and scalloped and pleated pockets. Later still, another style of battle jacket (blouse) was introduced in an effort still further to reduce costs, conserve materials, and use labor more efficiently. This had two flat breast pockets, no lower pockets, and no skirt; it was of variable quality.

Breeches of good quality wool were issued with tunics early in the war, but they were later replaced by the simple straight-leg trousers, which were worn with either suspenders or a belt.

As the war took its toll on equipment and supplies of raw materials, quality declined everywhere. Initially uniforms had been well made and of good quality wool. By 1943 only average quality goods were being manufactured, and by 1945 all attempts to maintain quality had gone by the board. The only goal was to meet the needs of the military machine with whatever was available in the best way possible.

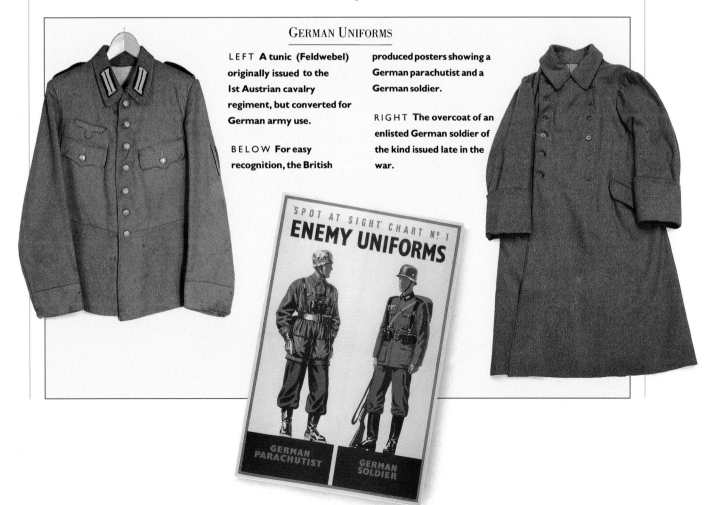

GERMAN UNIFORMS

LEFT **A tunic (Feldwebel) originally issued to the 1st Austrian cavalry regiment, but converted for German army use.**

BELOW **For easy recognition, the British** produced posters showing a German parachutist and a German soldier.

RIGHT **The overcoat of an enlisted German soldier of the kind issued late in the war.**

'SPOT AT SIGHT' CHART N° 1
ENEMY UNIFORMS

GERMAN PARACHUTIST

GERMAN SOLDIER

The Germans made good use of captured stocks of clothing obtained from the armies of the countries they occupied. Austrian army uniforms were re-cut and modified, as were those from Norway and the Netherlands. The invasions of Poland and France led to the capture of huge stocks of military supplies, and most of these were converted to conform as closely as possible to German regulations. Those that could not be changed adequately were issued to the Todt units and puppet state armies that the Germans controlled.

Because their uniforms were converted in this way, very few of the occupied nations' pre-war uniforms or uniforms from the early years of the war are available for collectors. Since many of them were dyed to resemble German uniforms, collectors tend to exhibit only restrained enthusiasm when someone tells them about a "field gray" uniform.

The Germans developed several light-weight uniforms for use in warmer climates. The first combat uniform for North Africa was a khaki cotton version of the wool uniform. The extremes of climate led to the khaki tunic and trousers being replaced with shorts and a long-sleeved shirt. Made of lighter weight material, the sleeves could be easily rolled up for added comfort. In addition, wool overcoats were issued for the cold desert nights and winds. This uniform was also issued in reed green.

In North Africa German soldiers often wore captured Allied uniform parts, adding German insignia. In addition, many non-standard materials were used, including corduroy, denim of various weights, and wool gabardine, but the majority of the uniforms still conformed closely to regulations.

Winter uniforms were made of wool, but service on the Eastern Front made new demands of German soldiers. Special uniforms had to be developed to meet the harsh winter conditions and to cope with the tactical problems found in that theater of operations. The new winter combat uniform proved so successful that it was used by German troops throughout Europe in the winter months.

GERMAN COMBAT UNIFORMS

LEFT **A tropical-issue tunic for the Luftwaffe.**

BELOW LEFT **German army corduroy tropical shorts.**

LEFT **Insulated felt boots of the kind issued to Luftwaffe air crews. These may be distinguished from those issued to soldiers on the Eastern Front by the lugged soles.**

LEFT **German army field marching boots.**

The Germans also developed a camouflage uniform, as well as a number of excellent dual-purpose uniforms, most notably the quilted, reversible parka, which was white on one side and had a gray or camouflage pattern on the other. The camouflage uniform was changed continuously, both in pattern and design, and as a result, no single uniform achieved universal use throughout the armed forces. Acquiring a complete set of all the varieties presents a challenge for the collector.

German boots were the traditional-style field marching boot (jackboot) with hob nails, hoof irons, and, sometimes, toe plates. The finish was either pebbled or smooth. Officers used the riding-style knee boot with similar sole protection. Mid-war material shortages led to the replacement of the jackboot by the short lace-up boot. This boot was usually worn with short leggings, fastened with a buckle. The short boot was also worn with old-fashioned puttees. Special felt and leather boots for use in winter and in cold climates were issued to ground forces. These had two types of sole – one was identical to that found on the field marching boot, and the other was of wood. Collectors should be aware that special boots were worn by Luftwaffe crews. They had leather soles and added leather lugs. Wooden-soled boots were issued primarily to soldiers assigned to sentry duty.

MILITARY DRESS UNIFORMS The German army had always prided itself on the appearance of its dress uniforms, and a new uniform, the Waffenrock, had been authorized just before the outbreak of hostilities. This was basically the traditional gray uniform but with the addition of colored piping to signify the branch of service. Trousers bore piping along each outside seam.

All ranks wore decorations on full dress uniform, while ribbons were worn on informal dress tunics and jackets (blouses) as occasion demanded. Full dress tunics had no external pockets. The informal dress tunic followed the same cut and design as the dress tunic, but the pockets were pleated, and the pocket flaps had scalloped edges. The standing collar of both the dress and informal dress tunics was dark green with collar tabs.

Trousers were worn by all enlisted ranks of the infantry. Breeches were worn by all officers when they appeared in full dress, and breeches were optional for officers in informal dress. Field boots were worn by all enlisted ranks for both dress and informal dress occasions. Although they were authorized, shoes seem to have been little used. Officers were required to wear riding boots and spurs when appearing in dress uniforms, but they were permitted to wear shoes when they appeared in informal dress.

Officers and high-ranking non-commissioned officers wore swords when they were in full dress. Many also wore daggers as an optional accessory when they were wearing informal dress uniform.

ABOVE **A German infantry officer's dress tunic.**

·········ITALY·········

COMBAT UNIFORMS Italian uniforms were made from good quality wool. They consisted of standard-issue tunics, antiquated breeches with puttees, and an overcoat of standard design. The early standardization of Italian uniforms and equipment, together with a lack of money and shortages of materials, meant that there were very few variations, even in the quality of materials used, throughout the course of the war.

The tropical uniform appears to have been slightly more advanced in design than those used by other combat forces, possibly as the result of lessons learned from an early involvement in Africa. Initially, Italian uniforms were patterned after the standard wool design, but made of cotton. Two colors were prevalent at the beginning of the war – slate blue-gray and white. The slate blue-gray uniform was preferred by most military personnel, particularly officers. The white tropical uniform proved to be highly ineffective when used in combat, partly because wounds suffered while soldiers were wearing that uniform were found to be especially demoralizing, partly because the general cut of the white tropical uniform restricted movement, and partly because staining and laundering problems made it virtually impossible for the soldiers to maintain a smart appearance.

The tropical uniform was copied to some extent by nearly every nation involved in the African campaigns. The basic uniform was made of cotton drill. The tunic and shirt were similar in cut, with open neck and an adequate number of vents to allow the movement of air. Shorts and breeches were available in the same material. The overcoat, which was wool, was issued in large quantities to combat the cold African nights and desert winds. Knee-high socks, an alternative to puttees, were worn according to the preference of the individual soldier.

The Italian uniform proved totally inadequate for troops assigned to the Balkans. The severe climate, difficult terrain, and diverse tactical demands of the area quickly revealed the inadequacies of the standard issue. Several quick-fix solutions were tried, one of which was a fur-lined vest, but a fur-lined vest alone cannot prevent frostbite of the extremities.

During the period of the Allied invasion of Italy the Italian military designed a camouflage uniform that proved to be well suited to the local terrain. German forces assigned to defend Italy also adopted this pattern. When cloth was available, uniforms were made to the Italian design as well as to the standard pattern for the German jacket (blouse) and trousers combat uniform.

MILITARY DRESS UNIFORMS The military dress uniform of the Italian enlisted soldier was extremely modest. Officers' uniforms, on the other hand, were much more elaborate. The basic uniform was of blue-gray wool. The stand and fall collar featured insignia to denote branch of service, while epaulettes indicated branch of service and rank. The shirt and tie matched the rest of the uniform in color but were made of lighter weight material.

The military dress uniform was accompanied by a green-gray leather belt and a steel roller buckle. The buckles of enlisted men were painted black. Officers wore Sam Browne belts in either the basic green-gray color or brown.

All ranks wore breeches. Enlisted men were issued with puttees or with leather leggings secured by a strap, catch, or laces. Officers usually wore riding boots.

Decorations were worn with the dress uniforms, and the Italians preferred ribbons to any other forms of adornment.

Collectors of Italian uniforms will find a tremendous range in the quality and cut of officers' dress uniforms. Many officers wore uniforms that were made by individual tailors, and even standard-issue officers' uniforms have a tailor-made quality. Almost the only way of distinguishing among them is to find a tailor's mark.

Of all the headgear and uniforms that can be collected, Italian examples are of consistently higher quality than those of all other countries in respect of both the cut and the materials. This is true for all ranks. The headgear and uniforms of Italian forces, especially of the elite troops, are eagerly sought by all collectors.

·················· JAPAN ··················

COMBAT UNIFORMS Japanese combat uniform, which included outmoded breeches or puttee-like trousers, were usually made of khaki cotton. The combat uniform was simple and modest in design and construction, and there is little to differentiate an officer's uniform from an enlisted man's apart from the quality of the tailoring, the material used, and the insignia.

The uniforms varied from pea green to deep brown, or from khaki to white. The buttons were plain. The two most often found combat uniforms are Pattern 90 and Pattern 98. An overcoat existed in both patterns, although collectors come across far more Pattern 90 overcoats than Pattern 98 coats.

Winter combat uniforms followed the same basic design as the summer uniform, but with the addition of a standing collar on the tunic and long trousers. Trousers are difficult to find, and are highly prized by collectors. Obviously many were the victim of hard campaigning, but it is equally possible that trousers were issued in only limited numbers.

Japanese personnel stationed in cold climates either purchased or were issued with large quantities of wool garments. That these garments were issued cannot be verified, but there is no doubt as to their

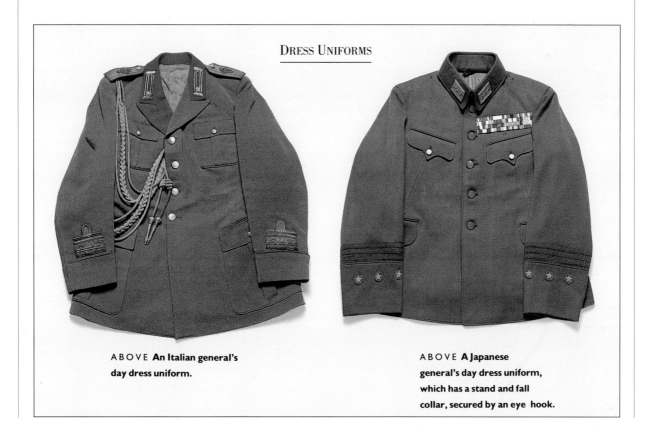

DRESS UNIFORMS

ABOVE **An Italian general's day dress uniform.**

ABOVE **A Japanese general's day dress uniform, which has a stand and fall collar, secured by an eye hook.**

use. Fur-lined vest jackets (blouses) in Pattern 90 were used in cold climates, together with quilted clothing of uncertain origin.

Japanese shoes varied from riding boots for officers and senior non-commissioned officers to sandals. The most unusual item of footwear – perhaps of the entire war – was a separately toed shoe, which was issued to soldiers assigned to jungle combat. It was flexible and had a natural rubber sole.

MILITARY DRESS UNIFORMS The military dress uniform, which was worn by all ranks, was very similar to the combat uniform, and, again, the only way of distinguishing between ranks is by the quality of material and the insignia.

There were two jacket (blouse) patterns, both of which had stand and fall collars. The older pattern had two breast pockets with a single, exposed button on each. The later style followed basically the same design as the earlier version, but it had four pockets. Officers wore a white shirt, while the military dress uniform for enlisted men required a khaki shirt. The shirt was, however, usually hidden by the standing collar of the tunic.

The tunics and breeches of both officers and enlisted men were of khaki wool. Rank insignia were worn on the collars, while ribbons were worn on the left breast above the pocket. Officers wore brown riding boots, while enlisted men wore short boots with puttees of khaki wool.

·············· UNITED STATES ················

COMBAT UNIFORMS Although US combat uniforms had changed significantly in design since World War I, the materials and colors were relatively unchanged. Some experiments had been done with a forest green uniform for cold-weather combat, but the results were not satisfactory. Isolated examples of pieces of this uniform may be found in several collections, but a complete uniform is rare.

The temperate-zone combat uniform consisted of a wool olive-drab shirt and trousers, black or khaki tie, web belt with brass buckle, khaki cotton duck leggings, brown shoes in various patterns, and a four-pocket jacket (blouse) with falling collar and pressed-back lapels. It was topped with a double-breasted overcoat of coarse olive-drab wool with a double row of brass buttons. A light khaki jacket (blouse) with a lightweight blanket lining – M1941 – was also issued, and accessories included a scarf and leather-lined gloves. This uniform was standard-issue throughout most of the war in Europe.

In 1943 a newly designed combat uniform was issued on all fronts. The herringbone twill uniform – HBT – consisted of a cap or hat, shirt, jacket (blouse), and trousers. This uniform was more durable and easier to launder under field conditions, but it was appropriate for hot and temperate climates only. When fighting occurred in cold climates the uniform had to be supplemented by long underwear and additional outer garments. The improved field jacket (blouse) made its appearance at this time, together with the fur-lined pile cap and parka.

Shoes were a major problem. Resources were limited, demand was massive, and each climate presented a different set of requirements. Many attempts were made to find alternative materials for use as soles and the upper portions of boots and shoes. None was widely successful. Most common were the double-buckle combat service boot and the service shoe or boondocker, and the latter was usually worn with leggings.

The 1941 tropical uniform left much to be desired. The chino (strong twilled cotton) uniform consisted of long-sleeved shirts and long-legged trousers. Breeches, which were extremely popular with officers in tropical postings, were available and issued to large numbers of troops. Shoes were the

US COMBAT UNIFORMS

LEFT **The herringbone twill hat and jacket worn by members of the US Marine Corps.**

RIGHT **The standard-issue US MI field jacket (blouse).**

ABOVE **Standard-issue US army underwear – shirts, shorts, and socks.**

ABOVE **US army field shoes.**

ABOVE **Herringbone twill trousers, with boondockers and leggings, worn by members of the US Marine Corps.**

ABOVE **US army khaki tropical shorts.**

LEFT **US army double-buckle boots.**

same as those issued to the rest of the army. Leggings of khaki duck with brass hardware were worn with most of the quartermaster-issued footwear. As the war progressed a new tropical uniform, based on the herringbone twill combat fatigues, was issued. Several variations were used, and contemporary photographs reveal that combat forces often mixed different styles together, depending on what items were available.

The field jacket (blouse) was olive-drab with four pockets and exposed buttons throughout. The jacket (blouse) had buttons on the back of the collar so that a cloth hood could be attached. Late in the war, gloves with leather palms or knitted wool mittens with separately knitted trigger fingers were issued.

Overcoats followed the traditional pattern and color scheme. However, metal buttons were replaced by plastic ones late in the war. Matching trousers were cut fuller and made to button into the uniform Eisenhower or "Ike" field jacket (blouse), which replaced the M41 pattern.

ABOVE **An enlisted man's US army standard-issue overcoat. The plastic buttons** **indicate that this coat was issued late in the war.**

The US version of the British battledress jacket (blouse) had exposed buttons and was made in Britain. It was designed primarily for field wear, but it was occasionally altered and adapted as a replacement for the dress jacket (blouse).

Camouflage uniforms were issued in 1943. There were two principal designs and two shades of color combination. The first design was a one-piece uniform, which quickly proved impracticable, especially when the soldier had to answer nature's call. It was replaced by a two-piece version. The first color combination consisted of a bright greenish-yellow and brown spot pattern, which was similar to the German camouflage pattern. This similarity made it dangerous for troops fighting in Europe, and a second color scheme that made use of a lighter shade of green with brown and yellow was introduced. This pattern was used by the Marines and the forces in the Pacific Theater, and it is found only in the two-piece uniform.

Specially designed uniforms were issued for units such as paratroops, ski troops, and armored personnel. These are rarely found, and are, therefore, highly prized by collectors.

MILITARY DRESS UNIFORMS The military dress uniform underwent numerous modifications during the course of the war as it was redesigned to be more functional as well as to reflect changes in fashion trends.

At the outbreak of war enlisted men wore visor hats with a brown leather beak and chinstrap. The jackets (blouses) had four pockets and folded-back lapels. Shirts were white cotton, and ties were black wool. Rank insignia were worn on the sleeve, unit designations were sewn on the left shoulder, and branch insignia were worn on the collar corners. Decorations were worn above the left breast pocket.

Brown leather garrison belts with brass frame buckles were worn over the tunics. Trousers were a

US DRESS UNIFORMS

LEFT **The dress jacket (blouse) of a US Marine Corps corporal.**

ABOVE **The dress cap of an enlisted man in the US army was poorly made. It was similar in style to the officer's cap, but had a stiff crown and peak. This pattern was discontinued after 1943.**

BELOW **US army officer's brown dress shoes.**

RIGHT **The tropical wool dress jacket and cap of a member of the US Women's Army Corps.**

BELOW **The dress jacket (blouse) of a woman yeoman of the US Navy WAVE.**

ABOVE **The dress cap of an officer in the US army would have been privately** **purchased from the quartermaster or from post exchange clothing sales.**

US DRESS UNIFORMS

LEFT **The dress jacket (blouse) of a second lieutenant in the 8th USAF.**

RIGHT **The dress jacket (blouse) of a technical sergeant in the US army, worn during the campaigns in China, India, and Burma.**

LEFT **The dress jacket (blouse) of a corporal in the US air force.**

ABOVE **The dress cap worn by enlisted men in the US navy. It was worn with a blue wool uniform.**

lighter shade of green, and were made from the same material as the coat. Shoes were brown leather oxfords; alternatively, field boots with khaki gaiters were worn. Contemporary photographs show that both forms of footwear were used.

The enlisted soldiers' military dress uniform remained the same throughout the war except for two changes – the "Ike" jacket (blouse) replaced the tunic, and branch service piping was added to the overseas cap.

Officers wore dark green hats that matched their coats and trousers. Breeches were used by mounted branches. Officers' shirts, which were of khaki wool, were worn with black ties. Brown leather Sam Browne belts were worn instead of the garrison belts of the enlisted men. Shoes were either brown oxfords or riding boots, according to the particular branch of service.

Officers could, however, choose among several uniform styles. One military dress uniform featured an "Ike" jacket (blouse) together with trousers in the traditional enlisted men's color, with an overseas cap piped with officer's braid. A second style featured a dark green jacket (blouse), which could be worn instead of the tunic. Dark green trousers were replaced by "pinks," gray trousers or breeches.

Photographs taken during the war reveal an almost endless variety of styles. It is as if the US forces dispensed with formal regulations when in the field – even Eisenhower himself occasionally appeared in non-regulation uniform.

USSR

The Soviet Union was unprepared for a protracted war in 1942. Still trying to recover from a bitter purge of its military, most of the Red Army was inadequately equipped in all areas, including uniforms.

COMBAT UNIFORMS A major uniform change had been introduced in the 1930s, and all ranks were wearing the new design by 1936. The combat uniform became a standard dark brown wool for winter use, and the same color in cotton for tropical wear. The standard tunic had a falling collar, two breast pockets, and a five-button front. These small buttons were exposed on some tunics, concealed on others. It is not certain if there is a distinct pattern change for this variation.

Because of the shortage of shoe leather for boots, breeches with puttees are often found. Britain and the United States attempted to help overcome this

deficit, and large quantities of shoes were shipped to the USSR under the Lend-Lease scheme after March 1941.

Overcoats were double-breasted and had large collars. In 1943 a new double-breasted overcoat with concealed buttons was issued.

MILITARY DRESS UNIFORMS Although they were issued, military dress uniforms were not commonly worn during the war. Enlisted men, non-commissioned officers and officers below the rank of general wore virtually identical uniforms. The tunic, which was made of green-brown wool, had a standing collar with five exposed brass buttons. The collar, cuffs, and epaulettes were piped in the branch color. Rank insignia were displayed on the collar and shoulder boards.

Breeches were dark blue, and officers' breeches bore piping along the outer seams. Both officers and enlisted men wore black field marching boots.

The headgear for the military dress uniform was a visor hat bearing the appropriate insignia. It was worn by all ranks. The hat was piped around the body and top seams in the branch colors.

The dress uniform had simple, clean lines, and a straightforwardly military appearance. There are, however, wide variations in quality, and collectors should be alert to these differences.

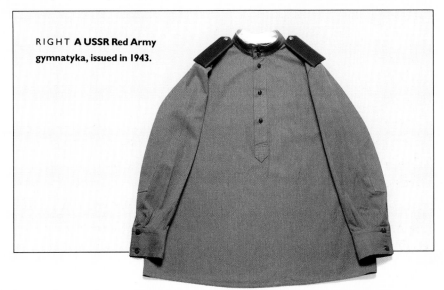

RIGHT **A USSR Red Army gymnatyka, issued in 1943.**

COLLECTING HEADGEAR

Headgear is an extremely popular area for collectors. It is readily available, found in a large number of variations, fits easily into a limited amount of space, and, in most cases, is extremely affordable. The survival rate is, moreover, surprisingly high, for headgear seems to have been retained long after other uniform parts have been discarded. One possible explanation is that many soldiers developed a personal attachment to – almost an affection for – their headgear, particularly if it had been used in combat. It is unlikely that you will be able to acquire an example of every piece of headgear used during the war, but if you divide the subject into four main areas – helmets, caps, hats, and oddities – you will be able to focus your efforts and build up a coherent and representative collection. You should always make sure that all the separate parts of each example of headgear – the correct chinstrap and liner, for example – are present and that the insignia correspond to the rank, branch of service, and the period of the war that the headgear is supposed to represent.

BRITAIN AND THE COMMONWEALTH The steel helmets worn by soldiers from Britain and Commonwealth countries were of similar design, and were superficially similar to those used in World War I, but they may be distinguished by the manufacturer's marks, which varied from nation to nation. The paratroopers' helmet differed from the standard-issue helmet, more closely resembling the style worn by German paratroopers. The suspension system was made of cloth instead of leather, and the chinstrap had a distinctive chin cup.

British and Commonwealth forces were issued with three different types of tropical helmet. The standard British pattern, which was worn on all tropical fronts, resembled a modified Wolsley pattern. The South African pattern helmet had a short brim and a wide puggree (the light scarf wrapped around the crown of a sun helmet and hanging behind to protect the neck). The Indian pattern helmet closely resembled a polo helmet.

The side cap was available in a variety of styles. One had external side flaps, and the buttons in front could be unfastened and the flaps let down to serve as a hood and ear flaps. The second variety resembled the first, but the sides were false and could not be used as a hood. The third version was a regular overseas-style flat cap with or without front buttons. Another form of side cap worthy of note is the Glengarry, which was the informal dress cap for all ranks in Scottish regiments. It had a band of tartan

ABOVE **The steel helmet worn by the British army was the same basic style that had been worn in World War I, although a few changes were made. The key points of** difference are the liner, chinstrap, and contractor – **World War II helmets have a black rubber liner with a khaki elastic chinstrap.**

ABOVE **Different colors and textures were applied to the basic British steel helmet when it was issued for duty in different theaters of operation.**

that identified the regiment, a cockade with the unit crest, and, often, ribbon tails. Some Scottish regiments wore the tam-o'-shanter or balmoral, an oversized beret with unit crest and in some cases a colored tassel or pompon on top, with both field and informal uniforms.

Many British and Commonwealth troops wore berets. A maroon beret identified paratroops, black, the armored divisions, and khaki, the infantry, while green denoted specialist units.

Officers used visor caps as hats. These caps had cloth brims and brown leather chinstraps, and they bore the crest of the branch of service or unit to which the officer belonged. Officers' caps in excellent condition are a welcome addition to any collection.

ABOVE **The khaki cap of a British medical officer.**

ABOVE **The steel helmet worn by Commonwealth troops was based on the British pattern but was manufactured in Australia. Canada, and New Zealand to** facilitate distribution to the troops. Manufacturers' marks are often the only way of identifying the national army concerned.

ABOVE **Berets were worn by members of the Canadian Army Transport Service. Different colors indicated different branches of service: khaki was issued to the infantry, black was worn by armored divisions, and green was worn by commandos.**

BELOW **The interior of a Canadian paratrooper's steel helmet.**

ABOVE **The helmet worn by Canadian paratroopers was designed to withstand greater shocks than other helmets and to allow the soldiers a greater degree of maneuverability.**

FRANCE The French continued to wear the World War I Adrian-style helmet during World War II, the 1916 and 1918 pattern helmets being used interchangeably.

French officers retained the traditional kepi (the cap with a horizontal peak), which was marked with the appropriate unit and rank insignia. The tropical headgear was the sun helmet. The *képi blanc* of the French Foreign Legion, was used by all ranks of the legion – officers, non-commissioned officers, and enlisted men alike. The side or overseas cap, which featured the branch color on top, was the preferred headgear throughout the war. It was used to complement the refitted US uniforms that were worn by the Free French.

ABOVE The French steel helmet continued to be produced in the Adrian pattern that had been used in World War I. However, the earlier helmet had been made in three pieces; the helmets used in World War II were made in two pieces.

GERMANY German military headgear is found in more patterns and styles than in any other nation. The quality is variable – early examples are often excellent, while later examples can appear quite shabby.

Two basic helmets were produced in the war, but special models were issued for various branches. The 1935 model helmet – M1935 – had a rolled edge; the 1943 model featured a sharp edge. Both styles had identical leather chinstraps and liners. Special helmets were made for the paratroopers and members of the Luftschutz. The paratroop helmet did not have the neck flange found in the standard helmets, although it did retain the rolled edge and the leather liner and chinstrap. Two gladiator-style variations of the Luftschutz helmet were manufactured. The one-piece helmet had a rolled edge; the two-piece helmet had a sharp edge. Liners were leather, although examples have been found with plastic or leather chinstraps.

The tropical helmet was issued in two styles. The first model, which was covered in khaki cotton, had a shield on each side and a leather chinstrap and liner. The second model was covered in greenish felt, and had a green leather chinstrap and natural leather liner. The insignia for both models was the same.

The three most commonly found soft caps are the 1938, 1942, and 1943 models. The 1938 model was made of field gray wool with no buttons on the front and no visor. The national cockade, the eagle, and the branch color were worn on the front. The 1942 model was similar in design, but it had two buttons on the front, which allowed the ear flaps to be buttoned under the chin. The cap was made in khaki cotton as well as in gray wool. The 1943 model soft cap was similar to the alpine mountain troop cap, but it had a longer peak. The Afrika Korps version of this model, which was made from khaki cotton, did not have two buttons on the front or ear flaps.

LEFT The 1938 model is the most common type of German steel helmet. It is seen with Heeresgruppe (army) markings.

RIGHT The German tropical pith helmet, second patterns, was also worn by Italian troops.

The soft cap worn by the alpine mountain troops deserves special mention. It served as the prototype for the 1943-style soft cap. Early alpine mountain troop soft caps had a short visor, but as the war progressed the visor lengthened until it was nearly identical in size to that of the 1943 model. The later alpine caps may be identified by the distinct green branch strip on the front that denoted mountain troops.

There are two versions of the peaked visor cap, which was worn by officers as well as by non-commissioned officers. One style had a leather peak and chinstrap; the second had no chinstrap and a peak made of stiffened cloth to match the color of the top. Because the insignia was the same for both the officer's and non-commissioned officer's peaked visor cap, it is important to note that an officer's cap tended to be of better quality, it had silver piping around the top and the branch of service color around the body, and the chinstrap was silver-colored cord rather than leather.

LEFT **The German M38 Feldmutz cap saw hard campaigning and is seldom encountered after 1944. It is often decorated with a V-shaped Waffenfarbe, a piece of colored cloth to indicate branch of service.**

ABOVE **This type of hat was worn by all German staff officers. It has a braided cord chinstrap, and colored piping** **was added around the crown and band to indicate branch of service.**

ITALY By 1939 the Italians had abandoned the 1918 Adrian-style helmet for the 1935 model bullet-head shaped, steel helmet with an unrolled edge. The helmet had a German-style leather liner and chinstrap. Occasionally, collectors find helmets with unit crests on the front. The tropical pith helmet also closely copied the German model. It can be found in white or khaki, with the national colors on the puggree.

The most commonly found Italian soft cap took its styling from the German 1943 model. The peak was slightly higher and the preferred fabric was blue-gray wool, the quality of which varied according to rank and whether the cap had been privately purchased. When used by troops in the tropics, the cap was made of khaki cotton. The headgear of the elite troops is especially popular among collectors. The alpine units, for example, wore a cap that was based on the traditional Tyrolean hat and was made of the finest wool felt, with the national crest on the front and a feather used to denote rank.

Italian officers wore a visor cap based on the French pre-war naval officer's hat. It had a large top, leather visor, and the national insignia on the front. When the Italians switched allegiance from Germany to the Allies the British helped outfit the troops. Italian headgear and uniforms were identical to those of the British, apart from the unit crest and rank insignia.

ABOVE **This pattern of steel helmet was adopted by the** **Italian military in place of the Adrian-style helmet.**

JAPAN One basic style of helmet was used throughout the war. It had a leather chinstrap and cloth liner, and it was often worn with a havelock (a cloth covering the back of the neck) and a helmet net. Occasionally a single star appeared on it.

Japanese troops in the tropics used a pith helmet, which was usually covered in white cotton. As with the helmet, some bore a single star.

All ranks of the Japanese military used the same style soft cap, which can be distinguished only by the quality of the cap – officers' caps were of better quality than those of enlisted men. The basic soft cap was made of wool or cotton, depending on the theater of operation. The only adornment was a single star and leather chinstrap. A havelock was often used with the cap as well.

The visor cap was based on the pattern that had been used in Europe in World War I. These khaki cloth caps, which were decorated with a single star and a red band and piping around the crown, had a leather visor, chinstrap, and sweat band. Some examples are lined with silk. The cap was especially popular with non-commissioned officers.

ABOVE **A rare cap of a Japanese non-commissioned officer.**

UNITED STATES US troops entered the war using an improved version of the World War I helmet known as the Gilley. The steel outer shell was virtually the same, but the detachable liner was now of leather on a spring steel frame. The khaki cloth chinstrap had a ball-and-lock catch.

The Gilley helmet was replaced by the M1 helmet. The first models had a liner made of cloth-covered paper and fiber that simply did not hold up well in the field, and a fiberglass-like material eventually replaced the paper and fiber liner. Both M1 liners had metal tits at each side to which the leather chinstrip could be attached, and the helmet was designed to accommodate a camouflage net.

In the tropics the army and other branches of the military used a cloth-covered pith helmet. Army helmets were usually khaki, while those of the Marines and the navy were plain green.

The US military used one variety of overseas cap, but the material used depended on the theater of operation. Examples are found in cotton, tropical wool, or wool.

At the beginning of the war the khaki caps of enlisted men had piping on the sides to indicate the branch of service. Officers' caps, which were piped with silver and black thread, tended to be made from dark forest green wool or wool gaberdine. As the war continued, the officers' caps retained the piping, but those of enlisted men became plain.

The visor hats worn by officers and enlisted men followed basically the same style, and collectors differentiate between them by the emblems. The emblem

LEFT **The early Gilley steel helmet saw hard campaigning in the Battles of Wake Island, Midway Islands, and the Philippines.**

RIGHT **The US army's Gilley helmet had internal webbing.**

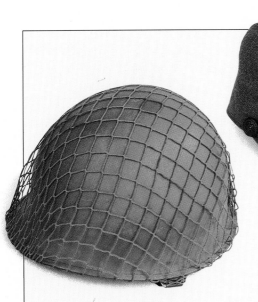

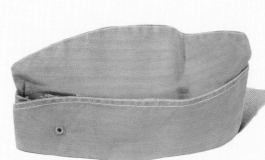

ABOVE **A hat of the kind worn by enlisted women members of the US Marine Corps.**

ABOVE **The first pattern US MI helmet – the "steel pot" – with camouflage net. This style, which is still in use, was copied by the French in the post-war period.**

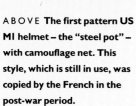

ABOVE **This rare campaign hat was worn by members of the US Signals Corps. Some veterans of World War I preferred to wear these hats when they were available.**

ABOVE **The overseas HBT garrison cap was worn by US enlisted men.**

ABOVE **The Marines were the only US troops to use a cloth camouflage cover on the MI pattern steel helmet. They also had cloth, not leather, chinstraps.**

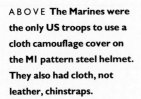

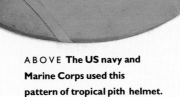

ABOVE **The navy's fire control teams used helmets with headsets for communication on board US vessels.**

ABOVE **The US navy and Marine Corps used this pattern of tropical pith helmet.**

used by enlisted men had an oval background, which is not found on the emblems on officers' hats. Officers' hats also had a ventilated headband or a green headband, which contrasted with the rest of the hat. Both hats had brown visors and chinstraps.

The Air Corps version of the officers' hat had no stiffener in the crown and a flexible visor. This hat is known to collectors as the "50 mission crush" hat. An extremely popular cotton herringbone fabric fatigue cap, which was worn with herringbone fabric uniform, was issued during the war in both a long- and a short-peak version. The short-peak version is the more difficult to locate.

ABOVE **The "50 mission crush" hat of an officer of the US Air Corps. The hat's beak was made of soft material so that it would bend and fold, and there was no stiffener board in the crown. It is shown here with the standard officer's insignia.**

USSR Although the 1940 pattern of Soviet helmet appears to resemble the Italian version, it is, in fact, much more like the US M1 helmet in construction. Before this new design was available, the Soviet 1936 model helmet had been based on the World War I Austrian M17 Berndorder helmet, but this had proved unpopular with the forces and had been withdrawn after 1943.

The visor hat and overseas flat cap, which was worn by all ranks, were little changed from their pre-war designs.

The Soviet 1935 cap, with its pointed center, long ear flaps, and star on the front, is perhaps the strangest of all World War II headgear. Collectors like to include an example in their collections as a conversation piece. The cap was eventually replaced by a winter cap with fur sides and front, which could be turned up in warmer weather. The Soviet star was attached to the front. Soviet women soldiers wore the same headgear as men, and all the headgear featured Soviet insignia.

······ COLLECTING UNIFORMS ·······

The military combat uniform was, of necessity, designed for heavy use. Few examples have, therefore, survived in excellent condition, and those that are found tend to be from the last few years of the war. Combat uniforms, were, in any case, quickly discarded for dress uniform when troops left the combat zone, which makes them rarer still.

Concentrate on assembling a complete uniform. Use photographs whenever possible – the ideal is to duplicate a uniform seen in a specific picture. You should also try to obtain copies of the regulations covering the style of uniform that interests you and use these as a guide in building up your collection.

Resist the temptation to collect bits of uniform from several countries. Keep your collection under control by focusing on a single nation's uniforms. If you want variety, collect combat uniforms that relate to specific climates or theaters of operation.

Some collectors have built extensive collections by focusing on one individual article – belts or shoes, for example – and headgear is a perennially popular subject.

Quality is an important consideration when it comes to collecting uniforms. Condition varies widely, but always strive for the best possible quality, replacing items as you are able to find better examples.

Whatever type of uniform you decide to collect, it is important that the items retain the appropriate unit and rank insignia. Research the history of the unit concerned and keep it with the uniform. This additional information can greatly enhance the significance and value of a collection.

FIELD EQUIPMENT

CHAPTER 2

Field equipment consists of a belt and harness containing ammunition pouches, a canteen, a bayonet, frog and scabbard, and, in some cases, an entrenching tool case. Gas masks were also occasionally issued, depending on the theater of operation. In addition, a backpack or rucksack was used to carry personal gear, cooking and eating implements, additional clothing, blankets, tentage and poles, sleeping bags, and all the other equipment needed to maintain the foot soldier in combat.

A B O V E **Belgian soldiers used the same model of** **canteen that had been issued in World War I.**

The individual items required varied from country to country, of course, and the equipment issued to individual soldiers varied as they moved into and out of combat zones. The field equipment discussed in this chapter is that used by the combat soldier.

A B O V E **The Canadian pamphlet *Do's and Don'ts*, which was issued to troops on the point of embarkation,** **was designed to help soldiers prepare to leave their families and homes, and to acclimatize to overseas duty.**

BRITAIN AND THE
········· COMMONWEALTH ·············

At the beginning of World War II the field equipment used by British regular and territorial regiments consisted primarily of Pattern 08 pieces, the basic items that had been in use during World War I. Because Pattern 08 equipment remained the equipment of issue for the Indian divisions that fought in North Africa throughout the war, collectors seeking early examples of British field equipment look to India as a key source. As the war progressed, Pattern 08 field equipment was replaced by Pattern 37 equipment.

The basic Pattern 37 web belt was 2¾in wide and had narrow cotton webbing straps. The hardware was brass or another metal that was not critical to the war effort. Most web field equipment was continually treated with blanco, a process that ensured that all webbing was a uniform color. Pattern 37 material was issued in two basic colors – khaki and light green – and by using different colors of blanco, soldiers could change their gear to green, desert sand, white, or grayish-blue.

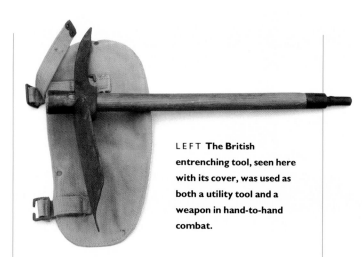

LEFT The British entrenching tool, seen here with its cover, was used as both a utility tool and a weapon in hand-to-hand combat.

RAF and naval Pattern 37 field gear was issued in the grayish-blue color, but few examples of this color equipment have survived, and they often sell for two or three times the price of an example in khaki or green. Learn to distinguish between the color tone of blanco-colored equipment and the original grayish-blue items.

One piece of field equipment that is worthy of special mention is the E-tool (entrenching tool), a combination cast pick and shovel blade, which was issued in two handle variations. The first version

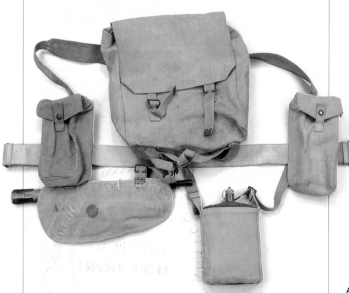

ABOVE Pattern 37 British field gear. This was colored by the soldier with blanco – green, sand, or grayish-blue – according to the theater of operation.

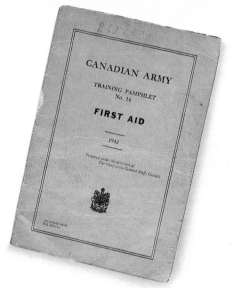

ABOVE A Canadian military first aid manual. Basic first aid was taught to every soldier to ensure that care and preliminary help could be given to fallen and injured comrades.

featured a plain wooden handle, but the second had provision for the attachment of a #4MK1 bayonet so that it could be used as a mine probe.

Commonwealth countries followed the British example, and as the Pattern 37 equipment became available, Commonwealth forces replaced their older gear, although not quite as rapidly as the British units. Some nations made minor changes to individual items – the Canadian canteen differed from the British frame type, for example – but the changes were slight, and British and Commonwealth nations' gear was largely interchangeable.

ABOVE **A pack of RAF playing cards (top left) and (top right) a game devised for** **British air crews to help them recognize enemy craft.**

···············FRANCE···············

Like the British, French field equipment at the beginning of the war followed World War I models, the principal kit being based on a 1916 pattern. A 1935 pattern kit was developed, although it was issued primarily to troops stationed in France.

Much equipment was lost or abandoned following the German invasion, and the Vichy government used what remained to equip the military during the period of the occupation. Vichy forces in Morocco and other French colonies wore suspenders, belts,

and ammunition pouches that were made of a russet-colored leather. Tentage was the same basic pattern as in World War I, but the material was heavier and grommets were added. The backpack changed from a lightweight black material to a heavier brown fabric. The alpine pack, however, continued to be made in the 1916 pattern. German troops liked the design of the French alpine pack, and large stocks were captured when France fell and issued to German units.

Photographs taken of Foreign Legion troops stationed in North Africa show that they were equipped with field equipment of the 1916 pattern, apart from the gas mask and bag. Most troops were equipped with the 1935 model, which replaced the familiar World War I canister with a bag, a much more serviceable device. The French military had decided, however, that its soldiers should have the latest design.

Free French forces fighting in North Africa were also equipped with the 1916 pattern field gear. However, this had changed significantly by mid-1943, when the Free French were supplied with US equipment, and from that time until the end of the war there is no difference between French and US equipment.

BELOW **A two-piece French Adrian-style helmet, a Croix de Guerre, and a canvas bag, originally designed to carry a** **gas mask but, because gas was not used in World War II, actually used to carry personal equipment.**

GERMANY

Like the Allies, the German military used field equipment that was based primarily on World War I patterns. Leather equipment retained its earlier color until 1942, when all German armed forces leather equipment was dyed black. The motto on the belt buckle remained the same – *Gott mit Uns* – but the insignia was changed to the Nazi eagle and swastika. Aluminum buckles were replaced by steel buckles when aluminum was required for other purposes than military field gear.

The Y-straps were changed so that the ammunition pack could be quickly detached and so that only one set of straps was needed to hold the cartridge belt as well as the pack. German World War II cartridge belts are a little thinner than their

GERMAN FIELD EQUIPMENT

BELOW **The canteen and harness issued to the Afrika Korps was covered with cloth webbing instead of leather for greater durability.**

ABOVE **German Model 34 field gear was the most widely issued kind.**

ABOVE **The fur pack was popular with German mountain troops, who called it a "Tornister."**

LEFT **A German rucksack, blanket roll, and tent unit, seen here in the standard carrying configuration.**

RIGHT **A German canteen, cup, and harness. When they could obtain them, most soldiers carried two canteens, both of which would have been attached to the Model 34 field gear.**

ABOVE **German tropical and standard-issue bread bags. The tropical issue was used by the Afrika Korps.**

World War I counterparts; otherwise the same.

Canteens were made of aluminum, covered with felt, and surrounded with a leather harness, which also attached the cup to the canteen. During the early stages of the war canteen cups were made from aluminum. As the war progressed, aluminum was replaced first by enameled steel and later by plastic. A bakelite canteen with a harness of cotton webbing was used in the tropics. The weather and a shortage of leather made it necessary to use cotton. Examples of bakelite canteen units are very difficult to find.

The standard-issue, hair-covered pack was closely modeled on the pack used in World War I. A later canvas version also drew its inspiration from the World War I model. The rucksack or alpine pack was based on the French pattern, using the same suspenders as the standard-issue 1934 and 1937 German versions. Although wooden assault frames were made in considerable numbers, they were subjected to hard use, and few have survived. The frame provided additional support so that a greater load could be carried.

The German army primarily used one model of shovel – a steel shovel blade mounted and riveted to a hardwood handle with a pronounced ball end. A later design for a folding shovel was similar to the US folding shovel, but it was not as sturdily constructed.

German-made tentage is found in two colors – gray and camouflage. Several camouflage patterns were used, the most commonly found being the green-tan water pattern used by the army. Many German units, however, carried tentage that had originally been made for the military of the countries they occupied.

The Germans were adept at using captured military stock. Large quantities of Polish, Austrian, Czechoslovakian, and French equipment were issued to German military field units, and collectors look to Germany as a source not only for German military gear but for that of other armies as well.

Many collectors believe that the reunification of Germany will open many sources in what used to be East Germany that were previously closed to collectors in the West. If large quantities of new material are found there, there could well be a temporary fall in prices until the market has absorbed the new items.

ITALY

Italian field equipment underwent several model changes between the two world wars. Although some of the equipment was significantly improved, many items still left much to be desired. The typical strap suspenders and belt were of gray-green leather, and although canvas gear was issued to troops serving in a tropical climate, it was not always available, and leather gear may occasionally be seen in photographs of Italian troops stationed in the tropics.

One piece of equipment that was improved from the World War I pattern was the canteen. The World War II model was made of aluminum, and it survived the stresses of combat far better than its earlier counterpart. The canteen, which was not accompanied by a cup, was covered with the same material that was used to make the uniforms. The one major drawback was that the single strap and snap suspension system were clumsy, and the canteen tended to strike against the soldier as he marched.

The camouflage pattern used on Italian tentage was unique. German forces fighting in Italy found the pattern very effective, and they copied it onto their tentage as well as adopting it as the prototype for later German camouflage uniforms.

The pack in general use among Italian soldiers retained its World War I appearance, but the alpine pack was modified. The Germans admired and copied the new design, as they did with the French alpine pack.

JAPAN

The Japanese invasion of China provided a testing ground for existing Japanese field equipment, which, in the late 1930s, was largely based on German World War I patterns, albeit in somewhat simplified form. The equipment underwent a continual process of redesign and refinement throughout the war.

The soldier's leather belt and cartridge boxes were modified versions of the German Pattern 88 commission rifle box and belt. Whenever possible, leather was replaced by cloth, which the Japanese found held up better in combat. The stamped German belt plate was replaced with a simple japanned steel roller buckle.

The style of the Japanese bread bag was also based on the German pack, while the shovel was a cross between British and German designs. The Japanese modified the basic French design for their gas mask and bag.

BELOW **A Japanese aerial artillery observer's 1910 pattern instrument.**

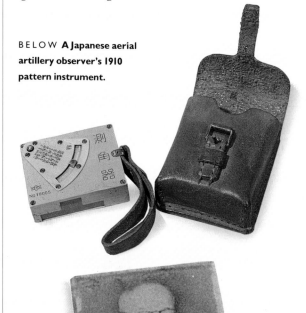

UNITED STATES

Several design changes were made to US field gear between 1920 and 1940, and new designs continued to be developed during the war as attempts were made to conserve materials, lighten the overall weight, and improve the method of distribution. US gear was also issued to the Free French forces.

The 1928 field cartridge belt and pack introduced modest improvements to the 1910 pattern field equipment upon which they were based. The packs were designed for specialized use, and two models worthy of note are the Marine Corps 1941 model knapsack and haversack, which could be combined as a single unit or used separately, and the 1936 model mussette bag, suspenders, and cartridge belt. A pistol belt in place of the cartridge belt was also available in the 1936 model. Another specialized pack type, the 1945 model, was a rucksack and frame, which performed far greater service during the Korean War than in World War II.

The khaki shelter half that had seen service in the 1920s and 1930s was redesigned to include end flaps, which afforded greater protection from the weather, and was issued in olive-drab. The earlier design for the canteen, cup, and cover was retained, but the canteen was manufactured in other materials – steel, enameled steel, and even plastic. The canteen caps were made in aluminum, then in plastic, and later in steel. Once again, khaki gave way to olive-drab for the canteen covers.

US forces often carried a first aid pouch as part of their standard field equipment. This Carlisle pouch changed little from its World War I cousin, although the earlier tin or brass box was replaced by plain cardboard. A snap fastener (lift-the-dot) allowed the pouch to be opened quickly.

The gas mask was an improved version of earlier masks. The bag was modified so that it was no longer located in the center of a soldier's chest during combat. Instead, the new model allowed the soldier

US FIELD EQUIPMENT

ABOVE The web belt with accessories worn by officers and crew-served personnel of the US army. This pattern was standard issue for most branches, and the web belt was the basis of all load-bearing equipment.

ABOVE The MI carbine magazine and pouches issued to US troops. The box magazine held 15 .30 caliber rounds, and it was not until the Korean War that extended magazines capable of carrying 30 rounds were available.

BELOW Model 28 field gear of the kind used by US infantrymen. This design was replaced by the 1945 field pack.

ABOVE A US army rucksack on a tubular frame of the kind that was usually used with a primary branch of alpine-trained troops. This particular example would have been used by the US 10th Mountain Division.

ABOVE The US M1945 field pack saw heavy use in all theaters of war.

BELOW Three US accessory pouches. At the top is a small arms accessory pouch, while the two lower examples are .45 caliber magazine pouches for use with models 1911A1 and 1911.

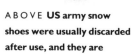

ABOVE **US** army snow shoes were usually discarded after use, and they are therefore rarely seen in collections.

to place the bag either under his left arm or at his side, depending on the type of work being performed. The khaki canvas bag was rubberized for use by the troops involved in the Normandy landings in June 1944, and this special variation is keenly sought after by collectors. Equipment designed for a single operation or series of events frequently commands premium prices.

When the war began, US troops used a short, T-handled spade or shovel, which was housed in a khaki cover. This was replaced during the war by a shovel with a folding handle and an olive-drab cover.

ABOVE **The US army found** the field radio, seen here with its case, effective for short- distance transmissions. In good conditions its maximum range was about 5 miles.

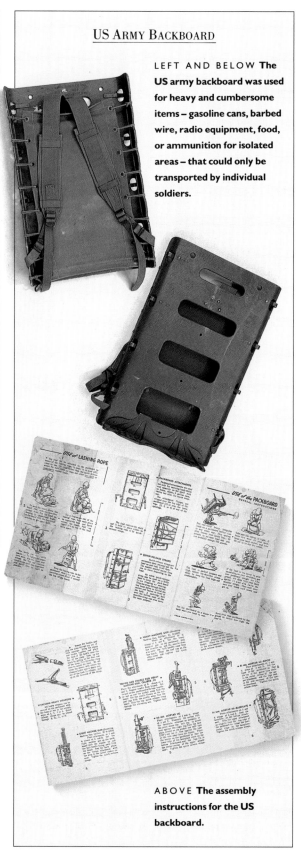

US ARMY BACKBOARD

LEFT AND BELOW **The US army backboard was used for heavy and cumbersome items – gasoline cans, barbed wire, radio equipment, food, or ammunition for isolated areas – that could only be transported by individual soldiers.**

ABOVE **The assembly instructions for the US backboard.**

USSR

Soviet soldiers were issued with a minimum of field equipment. Ammunition belts were leather or web cloth, with simple roller buckles or black-painted iron-frame buckles. Two types of cartridge box were in use. The first, a simple single-pocket pouch, was an exact duplicate of the World War I box, but the second, a two-pocket pouch, was not manufactured until the 1940s. These later, two-pocket pouches were made in both cloth and leather.

Packs were made of an olive green canvas, and both the rucksack and knapsack issued to Soviet soldiers had suspenders similar to the German World War I packs. Packs saw limited use, however, as Soviet troops preferred to use blanket rolls to carry their gear rather than to deal with packs and their support systems.

German World War I field equipment also served as the model for several other pieces of Soviet gear, including the canteen, shovel, and shelter tent. With only a few exceptions, all Soviet field equipment is olive green.

COLLECTING FIELD EQUIPMENT

One of the most interesting ways of collecting field equipment is by object type. A collection organized on these lines offers unique opportunities for comparing and contrasting the design and manufacturing capabilities of the countries concerned, and the differences are remarkable.

Collectors should also attempt to acquire design variations from different periods with a nation's output. A collection of this kind will reveal how different countries responded to changing sources of raw materials at different stages of the war.

Whatever the main organizing principles of the collection, however, every collector should attempt to acquire at least one complete set of field gear. As well as the intrinsic interest and value of the set itself, this is a valuable and salutary reminder of the weight of the equipment that individual soldiers were required to carry as well as of the large number of separate items of which they were expected to keep track.

LEFT **An assortment of compasses (from the left): a US Marine Corps prismatic compass; a US general-issue magnetic compass; a German lensatic compass; a German magnetic march compass; a US lensatic compass; and (below) a British wrist compass.**

RIGHT **Belt buckles: (top row, left to right) British RAF, Russian navy, German Labor Corps; (second row, left to right) US Marine Corps and army fatigue buckle, US Marine Corps dress buckle, German enlisted soldier's buckle; (third row, left to right) US army 2nd Division dress buckle, US army dress buckle, Japanese navy, Japanese marine; (bottom row, left to right) US army dress buckle, US Marine Corps dress tunic buckle, US army officer's dress tunic buckle, German political buckle.**

SMALL ARMS

CHAPTER 3

A small arm may be defined as any weapon that an individual soldier can carry or operate. The basic weapons of the soldier in World War II were the rifle and pistol, and at the outbreak of war such weapons were largely single action, bolt action, or double action. The term long arm is used by collectors to cover all firearms fired from the shoulder or from the cheek. Such weapons usually have long barrels and stocks (as on muskets), but the term is used for other firearms as well.

It is important to distinguish between small arms and squad and crew weapons, which are special weapons that were issued on a limited basis only. Such weapons are collected, but they are not discussed in this book. The remainder of this chapter is devoted to the weapons of the individual combat soldier.

Collectors should note that small arms are usually identified according to the marking patterns that appear on the weapons. These designations are rendered here in the form in which they appear on the weapons themselves.

BRITAIN AND THE COMMONWEALTH

In 1940 Britain and Commonwealth countries were largely armed and equipped with the same basic small arms that they had used in 1918.

The main infantry weapon was the SMLE #1MKIII with a 16in blade bayonet (SMLE stands

ABOVE Nicknamed "Big Ugly," the British .455 caliber Webley remained in service throughout the war although it was, technically, obsolete.

for short model Lee Enfield). This bolt-action rifle had been developed in 1903, but it was so efficient that it was kept in service until well after World War II, even though more advanced weapons were designed. The Enfield #4MKI, which had a spike bayonet, for example, was lighter and easier to mass-produce. The MKV jungle carbine was designed especially for use in the Pacific Theater, although it also saw limited commando use in Europe.

The Sten gun, particularly the MKII, deserves special mention as a personal small arm since it was not a crew-served or squad-level item. These cheaply made carbines, which used a 9mm cartridge, fired either single shots or full automatic bursts. Although accuracy was unreliable over 50ft, Sten guns were made in vast quantities and supplied to underground forces throughout Europe. In addition, because of its low cost and ease of manufacture, the design was copied by several other countries, including Germany.

British arms, especially the Enfield SMLE #1MKII and #1MKI, were also used to equip Belgian, Czechoslovakian, Norwegian, Polish, and other nations' forces in exile. Most of these weapons did not receive any additional markings, and it is not, therefore, possible to identify the individual country or unit that used the weapon. If additional marks were used, they were usually placed on the stock.

The side arms used by British and Commonwealth forces were much more varied in design. The most commonly issued side arms were the Webley .455 and .38 caliber revolvers and the 38 Smith &

Wesson. Canadian troops used the Browning and the Model 10 Smith & Wesson Victory, and the Australian government purchased many of these weapons for their own troops. The Browning used the same caliber ammunition as the Sten gun, but it was an exception, and the large number of calibers in use must have caused serious problems for the quartermasters.

Many US-made weapons were sold to the British armed forces under the Lend-Lease agreement. These arms were a mixed lot. Large quantities of Model 1917 30-06 were sold to Britain, but because they used a different caliber ammunition from most standard-issue weapons, they were distributed primarily to units of the Home Guard. The rifles were painted with a red-white-red band around the stock to indicate that they required special ammunition. Quantities of Model 1903 30-06 rifles were also sent to Britain, but most of these were destroyed after the war.

Britain was desperately short of weaponry, and many Colt 38 Specials and Model 38 Smith & Wessons were sold outright. These US weapons were stamped with British proofs, but again, most were destroyed after the war, and few have survived.

After Dunkirk many Americans donated personal firearms and optics (telescopes and binoculars) for use by civil defense organizations in Britain. Many of these items were lent on the understanding that they would be returned after the war. Few were, however, and collectors may occasionally find one of the US articles, stamped with British proofs.

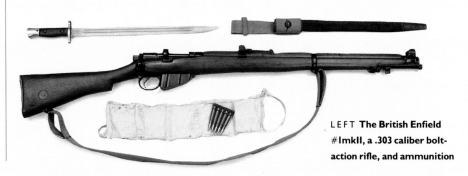

LEFT **The British Enfield #1mkII, a .303 caliber bolt-action rifle, and ammunition bandoleer with a stripper clip, together with the bayonet and scabbard. The MKIII was often made by Commonwealth manufacturers.**

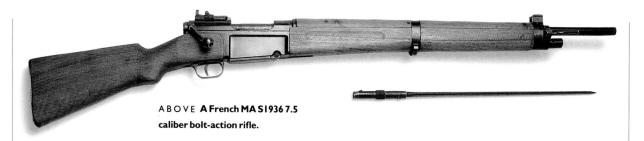

ABOVE **A French MAS1936 7.5 caliber bolt-action rifle.**

FRANCE

After 1940 French small arms played only a minor role in the war. The universal shortage of arms meant that those French small arms that were available were used by French colonial troops, members of the Resistance, and German Volkssturm and rear-echelon troops, but, as the war progressed and supplies of ammunition dwindled, their use declined sharply.

The long arms widely used by the French in 1940 were the 1886, M93, R35 rifle or the earlier Model 1886, which took 8mm Lebel cartridges. Both were equipped with 18in cruciform bayonets. Before the outbreak of war, the French had been in the process of modernizing the small arms used by their forces, but lack of funds and government foot-dragging had prevented the complete re-equipping of the military, especially the large number of reserve units.

The French MAS1936, a bolt-action rifle, was designed to accept the same caliber ammunition as the French machine-gun in order to reduce the logistical burden of ammunition supplies. Although the 7.5 caliber conforms closely to the .308 NATO round, they are not interchangeable. The MAS1936 saw excellent service with the Free French in North Africa, notably in the hands of the Legionnaires at the Battle of Birhakeim in May 1942.

After 1941 most Free French forces were equipped with arms and material from the United States, although they also used whatever weapons came to hand, including civilian arms, captured German arms, old French weaponry, and thousands of British Sten guns.

During World War II the side arms used by the French tended to be World War I revolvers or Spanish weapons such as the Ruby. Most wound up in the hands of the Germans or the Resistance. Fewer than 2,000 of the Model 1935S, an improved design, were produced, and the German occupation curtailed the distribution of those that were made. The Model 1935S used a 7.65 long cartridge, a bastard round, that prevented the weapon from gaining popularity, even among the Germans.

GERMANY AND THE OCCUPIED COUNTRIES

German World War II small arms are renowned for their quality and flawless performance. Despite the shortages of materials and manpower and the Allied bombing raids, the quality of German arms was maintained throughout the war, and manufacturers showed great ingenuity in salvaging weapons for reuse and in overcoming shortages of materials.

ABOVE **A French model 1935 A from which the model 1935 S was designed.**

GERMAN ARMS

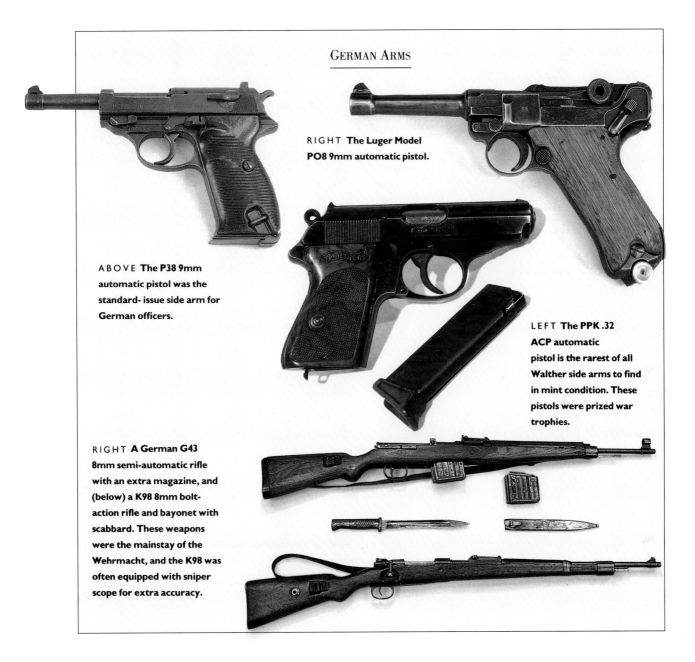

RIGHT **The Luger Model PO8 9mm automatic pistol.**

ABOVE **The P38 9mm automatic pistol was the standard- issue side arm for German officers.**

LEFT **The PPK .32 ACP automatic pistol is the rarest of all Walther side arms to find in mint condition. These pistols were prized war trophies.**

RIGHT **A German G43 8mm semi-automatic rifle with an extra magazine, and (below) a K98 8mm bolt-action rifle and bayonet with scabbard. These weapons were the mainstay of the Wehrmacht, and the K98 was often equipped with sniper scope for extra accuracy.**

As the war progressed Germany developed several semi-automatic rifles in response to the increased fire power of the Allies. The GEW 41 and the K43,G43 rifle may have been primitive in design, but they were highly effective. The principal problem with the weapons was the tendency for small pieces to break off and be lost during cleaning.

Side arms maintained the same high standards as German long arms. The P08 Luger had proved its worth during World War I, and the model remained in production until 1942. The P38, which replaced the P08, was easier to manufacture, and it met the demand for a side arm that fired more rapidly.

Many other side arms were adopted for war use, especially for rear-echelon troops and Todt organizations. The Model 1914 Mauser enjoyed considerable use as a side arm in both world wars, and the Mauser HSc was prized for its quality and reliability. The Sauer Model 1913 and Model 38H were preferred by Luftwaffe personnel, and the

Walther PP and PPK pistols have achieved fame
with side arm enthusiasts throughout the world.
War-time models differed from those used in peace
time in the color of the bakelite grip and the quality
of the finish. The caliber of most of the secondary
German side arms was 32 ACP, although some used
9mm kurz (380 ACP) cartridges.

The standard long arm of the German armed
forces was the K98, which had a 10in knife-blade
bayonet and either a wood or bakelite grip. The K98
was used by many of the armed forces of the
occupied countries, and captured military supplies
greatly increased German supplies. The increasing
demands for modern arms on the war fronts meant
that obsolete military and civilian weapons of all
makes and calibers were used within Germany itself.
Luftwaffe air crews were sometimes given Drillings
as survival weapons; weapons used for this purpose
are stamped with Luftwaffe proofs. Many members of
the Hitler Youth and the Volkssturm were armed
with obsolete military weapons such as the 88
Commission rifle, the Model 71/84, and, in some
cases, earlier percussion model muskets.

Collectors of German World War II weapons
should focus on German long arms and side arms
manufactured at almost any time between the late
19th century and 1945. It is difficult, however, to
document the use of earlier weapons in the war
unless they are proof stamped or have been carefully
documented.

AUSTRIA Austrian long arms did not conform to
German standard models, and Austrian weapons
were handed over to Hungary and other satellite
countries such as Croatia when they entered the war
on Germany's side. Austrian factories making the
Mannlicher service rifle were converted to produce
the German K98, although some Mannlicher rifles
were modified to accept the standard German
cartridge. Production of the 8×56R round for the

ABOVE **The 1912 Steyer
Mannlicher was usually
reworked to take the 9mm
parabolic ammunition used
by the Wehrmacht.**

Austrian Mannlicher service rifles continued
throughout the war, and some of these weapons were
distributed to the Volkssturm and other secondary
German forces.

Austrian handguns were quickly taken over by the
rapidly expanding German armed forces. The M1912
Steyer was converted to take 9mm Luger
ammunition, which was the standard for German
pistols, although those used by secondary forces
continued to take existing stocks of ammunition. The
M1912 Steyer was prized for the high quality of its
fit, finish, and functionality.

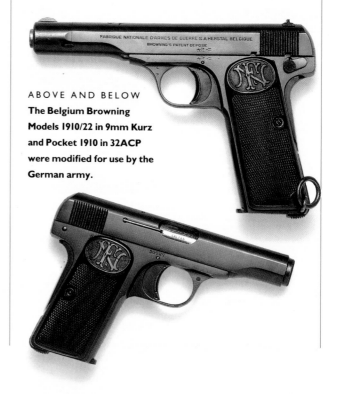

ABOVE AND BELOW
**The Belgium Browning
Models 1910/22 in 9mm Kurz
and Pocket 1910 in 32ACP
were modified for use by the
German army.**

BELGIUM The greatest German prize in terms of small arms was Belgium, whose arms manufacturing industry was led by giants such as Fabrique Nationale. Belgian armed forces were equipped with Model 24 Mausers, which had enjoyed worldwide sales before the war. The Model 24 Mauser was easily integrated into the German war machine, either as found or with minor modifications. The Belgian Browning Models 1903, 1910, 1922, and High Power were all modified for use by the German forces.

CZECHOSLOVAKIA Captured Czechoslovakian arms were valued for their quality and the ease with which they could be adapted by German military forces. The Model 24 rifle, which was used by 11 German divisions, remained in production after being modified to conform to the K98. Czechoslovakian pistols were manufactured throughout the German occupation, and the CZ 27 side arm was modified to increase the speed of production.

DENMARK Denmark had little to offer the occupying German military in terms of small arms. Those that were found served primarily as war trophies or were used for minor auxiliary forces.

THE NETHERLANDS The armed forces of the Netherlands were equipped with old World War I vintage Mannlicher design 6.5 caliber rifles. The Germans found these to be of little value except for guard use. Dutch side arms were mostly World War I vintage revolvers, which had been bought from Belgian or German manufacturers. These were found in only small quantities, and were readily absorbed into the Wehrmacht.

NORWAY Norway also contained few small arms that could be easily absorbed into the German war machine. The 6.5 caliber Krags were of value only to rear-echelon troops, but the Norwegian Model 1914 45 caliber pistol was prized by the Germans as a war trophy, even though obtaining suitable ammunition outside Norway was extremely difficult.

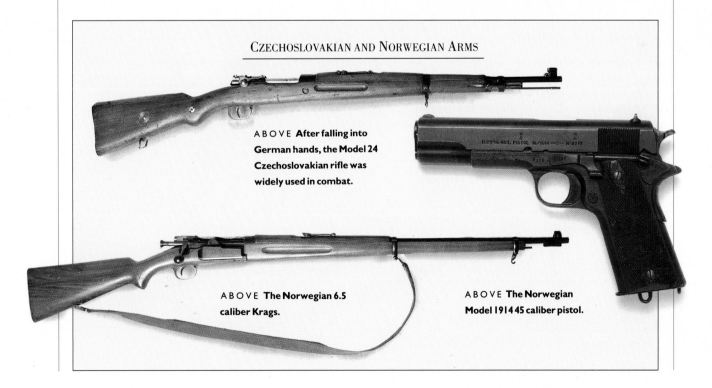

CZECHOSLOVAKIAN AND NORWEGIAN ARMS

ABOVE **After falling into German hands, the Model 24 Czechoslovakian rifle was widely used in combat.**

ABOVE **The Norwegian 6.5 caliber Krags.**

ABOVE **The Norwegian Model 1914 45 caliber pistol.**

ITALIAN AND POLISH ARMS

ABOVE **The Glisenti pistol produced by the Italians prior to the war.**

ABOVE **The highly successful Beretta 1934 pistol 380 caliber.**

ABOVE **A beautifully preserved example of a Polish Radom pistol which fell into German hands during the Polish surrender.**

ABOVE **The Italian 792 Carcano converted to take German ammunition and with typically German side-mounted sling.**

POLAND Such large quantities of small arms and associated equipment were captured from Poland during the 1939 invasion that seven German divisions were equipped. The Polish Model 24 was identical with the German K98a, and an earlier model was very similar to the German World War I version of the K98. Polish Radom pistols saw service on all fronts in the hands of German soldiers.

ITALY

Italian World War II long arms were modified versions of the weapons that had been used in World War I. The small, ineffective 6.5 round was replaced by the 7.35. This modification did nothing to improve accuracy, because the Italians continued to use fixed sights that could not be adjusted to allow for wind or elevation. In North Africa Italian Carcanos were converted to take the German 7.92 (8mm) round more for logistical purposes than for any other reason.

Italian handguns, especially those produced before the war, were of much better quality than their rifles. Although the Glisenti pistol was of mediocre quality and had a performance record to match, Beretta pistols proved far more effective. They exhibited excellent workmanship, and were highly reliable and accurate. The 1938 Beretta .380 (9mm kurz) and the 32(7.65) commercial variants both performed well, but they lacked the punch of larger caliber weapons.

JAPAN

The long arms used by the Imperial Japanese forces consisted primarily of the 6.5 caliber type 38 rifle and carbine and the 7.7 caliber type 99 rifle. Several take-down variants of these types were also manufactured.

A variety of handguns was used by the Imperial forces. These ranged in both quality and performance from poor to excellent. The Nambu, both large and small frame, were generally excellent weapons, but they lacked power. The 7mm and 8mm cartridges did not penetrate well or produce the knockdown power required of a military side arm.

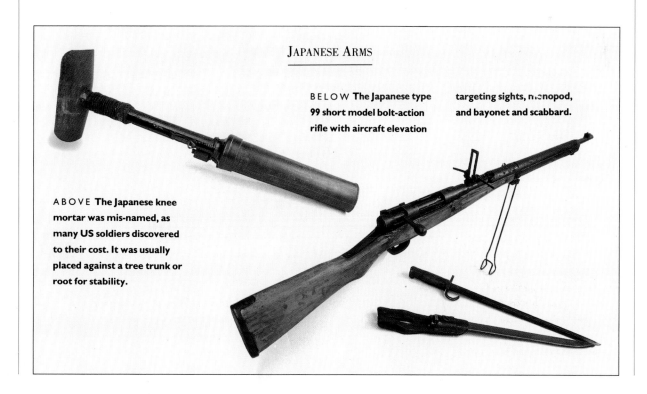

JAPANESE ARMS

BELOW The Japanese type 99 short model bolt-action rifle with aircraft elevation targeting sights, monopod, and bayonet and scabbard.

ABOVE The Japanese knee mortar was mis-named, as many US soldiers discovered to their cost. It was usually placed against a tree trunk or root for stability.

UNITED STATES

In common with most nations, the United States entered World War II using weapons that were largely based on World War I models. The 1903 Springfield, which used a 30-06 cartridge, was an adequate weapon in its day, but it lacked the rapid fire power needed to respond to the military tactics of World War II. The 16in bayonet with which the 1903 Springfield was equipped also proved inadequate – mass assaults and extensive hand-to-hand combat were rapidly becoming obsolete battle tactics.

US ARMS

ABOVE **The Springfield Model 1903 30-06 caliber with bayonet and scabbard was replaced by the Model 1903A3, which had** stamped (rather than milled) components and a rear peep sight (instead of a tangent sight).

ABOVE **The M1 Garand .30 caliber semi-automatic rifle gave US forces the edge that was necessary in personal combat. It is seen here with boxes of armor-piercing and ball ammunition, and accessory pouch, and (below) an M1 carbine .30 caliber semi-automatic with bayonet and scabbard, an extra magazine, and attached butt-stock magazine pouch.**

LEFT **This 37mm flare pistol and lanyard was used by all branches of the US military with a variety of flares – parachute, colored signal, ground assault and so forth.**

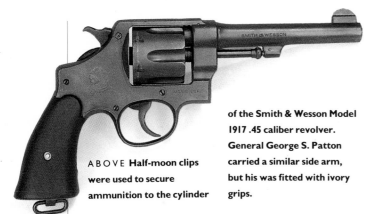

ABOVE Half-moon clips were used to secure ammunition to the cylinder of the Smith & Wesson Model 1917 .45 caliber revolver. General George S. Patton carried a similar side arm, but his was fitted with ivory grips.

Although the M1 Garand had been adopted in 1936, it was not manufactured on a large scale until 1942, but once wartime production started, large quantities were manufactured. The first M1 Garands were issued with a 16in Springfield bayonet, but this had been replaced with a 10in model by late 1942, and many of the 16in bayonets were altered by ordnance, field ordnance, or small arms repair units to conform to the new regulation size.

The 30 caliber M1 carbine was a supplemental weapon, which was designed to replace the pistol for front-line units or in situations in which weight and length were considerations. Although the rate of fire is impressive, problems occurred with firing performance, and rounds occasionally misfired. Initially the M1 carbine was not equipped to receive a bayonet, and soldiers carried the M-3 fighting knife.

The Johnson 30 caliber semi-automatic rifle is a variant rifle that performed effectively in the hands of the Marines during World War II, but it was not widely well received, and production ceased.

Most US pistols were 45 caliber. The 1911A1, which served as the main side arm throughout the war, performed superbly, being particularly effective in close combat. During the early years the 1917 Colt and Smith & Wesson models were used on a limited basis in the Pacific Theater, and they remained in use during the balance of the war.

US support troops also used several models of 38 Special revolvers. In most cases these weapons were military modified versions of civilian weapons. The military weapons can be identified by the parkerized finish and the addition of a lanyard ring.

USSR

The primary small arm of the Red Army was the Moisin Nagant rifle. The 1891 and 1891/30 models were crudely made but robust, and they were used for seven decades in various world conflicts. The Soviets used 7.62X54R ammunition in both the M1941 semi-automatic rifle and the 1891 model.

The 7.62 Nagant revolver was an oddity even in its heyday. The 7.62 Tokarev 1930 and 1933 models used different ammunition. Pre-war Mauser broomhandle commercial 7.62 ammunition was used when it was available, as was World War I ammunition.

Large quantities of weapons fell into German hands during their invasion of the Soviet Union. Rifles were passed along to the Slavic auxiliary forces, and some were turned against the Red Army by Vlasov's army. Only limited quantities of ammunition were captured, however, and it was issued sparingly. Little use could be made of captured side arms because the calibers were not compatible with German weapons, and because only limited quantities of ammunition were captured.

ABOVE The Red Army's Moisin Nagant 7.62X54R bolt- action rifle was used against Soviet forces by Finnish forces. The bayonet is a rare and highly desirable accessory.

THE SPOILS OF WAR

Weapons are among the most common of all World War II souvenirs. Although technically every weapon required some form of documentation, a great deal of discretion was exercised by many unit and division commanders, and most weapons that appear in today's collectors' market have no accompanying paperwork.

In addition to the weapons from a fallen enemy, World War II soldiers often returned home with their personal weapons. Favorites with US soldiers were the M1 Garand and M1 carbine rifle, and a 1911 Colt .45 pistol was regarded as a real trophy.

One of the requirements of the Allied occupation of Europe and the Far East was that all weapons should be surrendered. Although many were handed in and destroyed, a large number were hidden, and when Allied forces handed back the control of firearms to national governments, the enforcement of the requirements to turn in weapons became lax. Many of these arms have, over the years, appeared on the market.

Collectors acquiring one of these weapons should not fire it until it has been carefully checked by a gunsmith. Many combat weapons were used so heavily that stress has made them dangerous to operate.

Hand grenades or mines can be among the most dangerous of all World War II souvenirs that were smuggled home. Few soldiers would forgo the chance of obtaining a US pineapple fragmentation grenade or a German potato masher grenade, and the Japanese anti-personnel canister grenade was considered a major prize because so few survived, many Japanese soldiers using them to commit suicide rather than surrender.

Relatives of World War II service personnel have found grenades and mines along with uniforms and personal gear. These grenades and mines should have been de-activated before the soldier brought them home, but this did not always happen. If there is doubt, these items must be checked by the appropriate authority.

LEFT German hand grenades and rifle grenades. These items have been deactivated by trained personnel, and they are now used for study.

······ COLLECTING SMALL ARMS ······

It is possible to assemble an extensive collection of World War II artifacts and memorabilia without including small arms, but most serious collectors would regard such a collection as incomplete. Small arms were a major part of any soldier's gear – perhaps the most important part since his life often depended on his weapon – and no uniform is complete without the supporting small arm that was issued with it.

You should find out which weapons are common and which are hard to find – the US M1 Garand and the German K98, for example, are the most often found weapons. Study any small arm carefully before you buy, making certain that the weapon contains the proper parts of issue. Ideally, the serial numbers on all the separate parts should match. Unless you are collecting weapons on a regular basis, however, always seek advice from an established antiques or firearms dealer.

Prices for World War II small arms fluctuate. It pays to shop around. If you want a weapon only for display, you might be willing to accept an example with defects that a specialist gun collector would not, and if this is the case you will be in a position to save a considerable amount of money.

PERSONAL GEAR

CHAPTER 4

Personal gear, also known as personal issue equipment, includes items that soldiers used for personal hygiene and for the care and maintenance of their uniforms, small arms, and other equipment, as well as any religious items and personal necessities the soldiers carried with them. These items were obtained from a wide variety of sources, including the military supply companies that served the units, religious or charitable organizations, private purchase, packages from home, booty, or simply items picked up along the way.

Some military personal gear was viewed as consumables, and few records were kept of it after its initial distribution. Items for personal hygiene and the maintenance of equipment fall into this category. All military forces stressed the importance of personal hygiene – healthy soldiers were held to be more efficient soldiers – and in any case, a fit military force was good for morale. World War II military-issue personal hygiene items have survived in limited numbers, largely because soldiers were allowed to retain their personal gear when they were discharged, and they continued to use these items until they were exhausted. Collectors, therefore, seize every opportunity to acquire soaps, shaving creams and powders, toothbrushes and toothpaste, foot powders, and razors and razor blades.

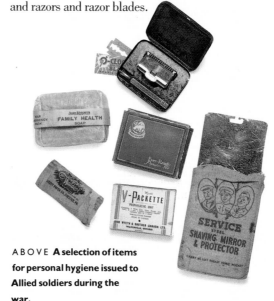

ABOVE **A selection of items for personal hygiene issued to Allied soldiers during the war.**

PERSONAL GEAR

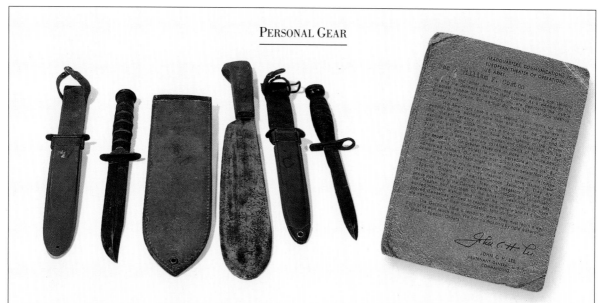

ABOVE **A collection of US fighting knives (from left to right): a navy K-bar, a Marine Corps smachett, and MI** carbine bayonet. These were made by various manufacturers and issued to individual soldiers.

ABOVE **A communication from headquarters for Allied soldiers in Europe explaining** in no uncertain terms just why the Nazi tyranny had to be defeated.

ABOVE **US army polishing cloth – "Zip" – was used to help keep uniforms spruce and neat.**

BELOW **Standard-issue US army sewing kit.**

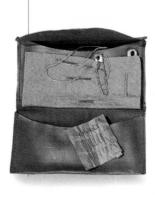

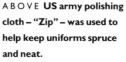

············ MILITARY ISSUE ············

Typical of the maintenance gear issued to troops are shoe dubbing and brass polishing kits, sewing kits (also known as housewives), and clothing marking kits. US, British, British Commonwealth, and German examples of these items can all be found, but examples from other nationalities are extremely scarce. For some of these forces, many of these items were regarded as luxuries.

PERSONAL HYGIENE It is not always easy to distinguish between an item issued by the military and a similar product made for the civilian market – German army-issue soap bars that were bought from commercial companies during the first years of the war were identical to civilian soap, for example. The British government had contracts with several soap and cosmetic manufacturers, including Yardley, but it is not known if Yardley was the only company making soap for the military under contract.

ABOVE **Assorted shoe dubbing cans – from the United States (top left and** top right), **from Britain (bottom left), and from Germany (bottom right).**

RIGHT AND BELOW **German and US standard-issue soap in its original packets.**

BELOW **German first aid bandages.**

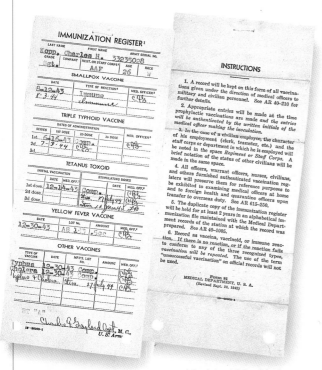

ABOVE **US military immunization records were needed to keep a check on a** soldier's health both before and after he was sent overseas.

Not all personal gear was obtained from the soldier's own country. Wehrmacht units used soap made by Dutch and Swiss manufacturers, and many of the bars still bore their civilian labels.

Some personal gear was of dubious origin. German troops on the Eastern Front complained about the brown, gritty soap that had no paper label. It has been suggested that it was made from the oil from human flesh, supply companies having to make do with whatever was made available to them.

Because the war was fought in a variety of climates around the world, personal gear often needed to be adapted if it was to work well. US naval personnel, for instance, were issued with a soap that supposedly worked well with salt water. Marines were not especially fond of this soap, and they traded it away or acquired other soap whenever they could.

As the war progressed and supplies of raw materials dwindled, countries were forced to economize. Initially, British and Commonwealth troops used soap that was commercially produced and wrapped, but later in the war soap was distributed without a wrapper, even though the commercial quality of the soap was maintained.

LEFT A selection of army issue foot powders. The favored 1¼oz was carried at all times. The pack was designed to keep the powder dry at all times and remains so to this day.

In an effort to reduce the amount of material a soldier was required to carry, attempts were made to develop multi-task products. British and Commonwealth troops participating in the North Africa campaign received a dual-purpose soap, which could be used for both bathing and doing laundry. Collectors who might want to consider starting a collection of soaps should be careful not to confuse dual-purpose soaps with the US Type II grit soap. This was a utility soap that was used for washing pots and pans and for maintenance cleaning; it was not for personal bathing.

The variety of personal gear that was issued enables collectors to assemble some unusual collections. It would, for example, be possible to concentrate on acquiring the soap dishes that were used by military units. British troops used two styles of aluminum soap dish – one hinged, the other unhinged – both styles are marked with a single broad arrow proof and dated. Although US soldiers did not have a military-issue soap dish, most soldiers chose to purchase a military-type dish, the two most popular choices being a sheet metal soap dish and an olive-drab plastic container.

US, British, and German forces were also supplied with towels. Most of these were of white cotton cloth, and they were very similar to each other. Often the only way to differentiate among them is by the fabric and pattern of fabric, technical data that are beyond the understanding of most collectors.

As far as dental hygiene is concerned, the item most frequently of military issue is tooth powder, which was supplied to almost all military forces. The only exception was the Red Army; to date, no records have been found to indicate that the Soviet military issued any dental supplies to its troops.

The military discipline of most armed forces required soldiers to be clean shaven, and great care was taken to see that shaving gear was available on all fronts. Only under extreme conditions were soldiers allowed to dispense with shaving – for example, when water was in short supply during campaigns in North Africa and during winter on the Eastern Front, when temperatures fell drastically.

Both commercial and military-contract razors and razor blades were provided to the troops. During the first year of the war, governments were prone to make large commercial purchases, but as the war progressed, contract purchases were more common. Two varieties of razor were issued – straight blade and disposable blade – and many bore the commercial logo of their manufacturer.

Surprisingly, although soldiers were expected to be clean shaven, most nations did not have a general-issue shaving soap. Shaving soap could be purchased privately in the ship's stores by British sailors, and US troops could obtain shaving soap through their post exchange. Many US military personal kits that have survived are found with a Rubberset pig bristle shaving brush.

BELOW Three-pair packs of US olive-drab army-issue socks, manufactured by Inter Woven Stocking Co. in 1942.

The novelty boxes for the utilitarian contents were designed to help boost morale.

A B O V E **Products for soldiers' personal hygiene were often manufactured by household names under contract to the military authorities.**

EYE CARE Poor eyesight might prevent a person from becoming a pilot, but it was no handicap to becoming a foot soldier, and soldiers requiring glasses generally carried at least one pair of military prescription spectacles. Most of the armed forces, Allied and Axis alike, provided a simple round wire frame with circular lenses.

Specialized glasses include the German *Masken-Brille*, which were designed to fit over the military-issue gas mask. Armies fighting in winter and tropical climates were often given polarized goggles or sunglasses. US pilots received two pairs of sunglasses, one with amber lenses and another with green lenses, both in a wire and plastic frame.

There is an old adage that an army travels on its feet, and the military tends, wisely, to pay a great deal of attention to foot care. Most armed forces issued foot powder when it was available, and containers are found in both commercial and military-contract packaging. Soldiers often complained about the ready availability of foot powder when items such as winter clothing and personal mail took "forever" to arrive.

Allied and Axis flight crews and bomber gunners wore protective goggles, as did ground vehicle operators working in the open air. It is quite common to find that the lenses of goggles worn by soldiers who fought in North Africa are fogged because of the abrasions caused by the sand.

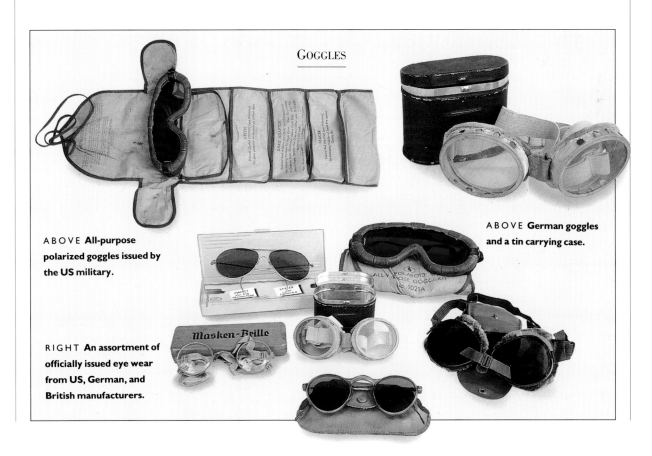

GOGGLES

A B O V E **All-purpose polarized goggles issued by the US military.**

A B O V E **German goggles and a tin carrying case.**

R I G H T **An assortment of officially issued eye wear from US, German, and British manufacturers.**

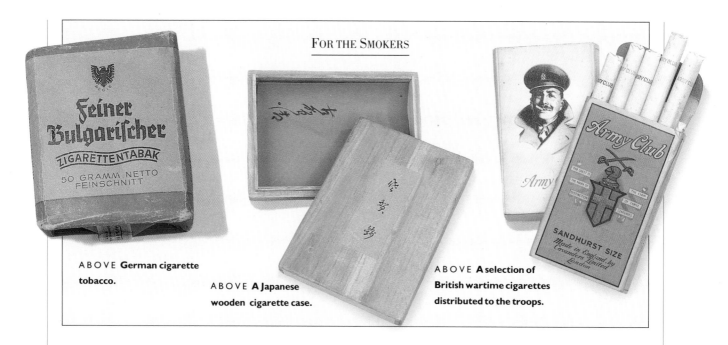

FOR THE SMOKERS

ABOVE **German cigarette tobacco.**

ABOVE **A Japanese wooden cigarette case.**

ABOVE **A selection of British wartime cigarettes distributed to the troops.**

CIGARETTES AND TOBACCO Smoking was a universal activity among soldiers of every nation. Early German military tobacco issues were left over from World War I – German veterans often recall the strong taste of this Turkish tobacco – although the soldiers actually preferred *Der Article*, a cigarette in an aquamarine packet. Players were the preferred cigarettes of the British troops, whose slang word for cigarettes – fags – passed into popular idiom.

American cigarettes were the most eagerly sought "smokes" during the war. The most popular brand among the troops was Lucky Strike Green, but all major US brands – Camels, Chesterfield, Philip Morris, and so on – were available. American cigarettes could be purchased at the post exchange or from the ship's stores. A real treat for many soldiers was a cigar, but they were hard to obtain, and often "care" packages from home were the only source of supply.

Matches were scarce, and soldiers relied primarily on lighters. American soldiers normally carried a Zippo or a Churchill service lighter, which are found in two colors, brown for ground forces and blue-gray for naval forces.

IDENTITY TAGS Every nation issued some form of identification tag to its military personnel. These tags are commonly referred to as dog tags, a term popular with US soldiers.

British and Commonwealth troops used a pair of heavy red and green pressed fabric disks. These were extremely strong, and they bore the name, serial number, and blood type of the serviceman or woman. They were worn on a white cord.

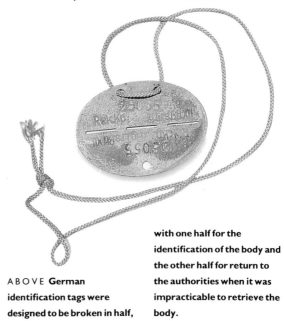

ABOVE **German identification tags were designed to be broken in half,** with one half for the identification of the body and the other half for return to the authorities when it was impracticable to retrieve the body.

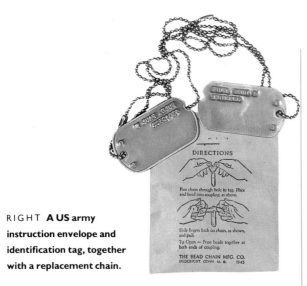

RIGHT **A US army
instruction envelope and
identification tag, together
with a replacement chain.**

German identification tags were made of
aluminum. They contained the name of the
serviceman, and his unit, serial number, and blood
type. The information was carried on both sides of
the two-part tag, so that half the plate could be
broken off for body identification if necessary. The
tag was worn on a cotton cord.

Italian identification tags were rectangular, and
they were made of brass and formed in two parts, one
plate resting over the other. The information
included the soldier's name, serial number,
birthplace, and parents' names. They were worn on
beaded metal chains.

Japanese identification tags were made of brass
and were oval in shape. They included the soldier's

name and unit, stamped in Japanese characters, and
they were worn on a white cord.

The US dog tag was a round-ended, rectangular
tag made of stainless steel. The tags were issued in
pairs and attached to a set of beaded stainless steel
chains. The metal surface of the tag bore the name of
the soldier, his serial number, blood type, and
religion.

RELIGIOUS ITEMS There is a close link
between military and religious institutions – soldiers
have always fought better when they have believed
that their god was on their side – and chaplains of all
denominations played a major role throughout the
war. Catholic soldiers were presented with scapulars
and rosaries, and many armed forces issued
religious items such as crosses, St Christopher
medallions, and printed religious texts. New
Testaments, printed and distributed by the military
authorities, were common. War had a strange way of
making everyone religious, and a common saying
among soldiers was that "there were no atheists in
foxholes."

In addition to the military and the established
churches, many charitable organizations distributed
religious items to the soldiers, often enclosing them
inside the good will and "care" packages that these
organizations sent to the troops.

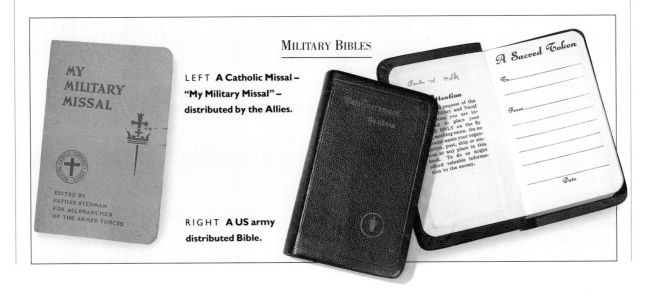

MILITARY BIBLES

LEFT **A Catholic Missal –
"My Military Missal" –
distributed by the Allies.**

RIGHT **A US army
distributed Bible.**

BELOW **By strapping this board game to the knee, the infantry were able to play a variety of games even on-the-move.**

PERSONAL ITEMS

Every soldier carried with him a host of family and other personal mementoes. Photographs of family, loved ones, and friends were tolerated, but not openly encouraged. Keeping a small personal diary allowed the combat soldier a few moments of quiet reflection each day, and many used the blank pages in their pocket testaments.

Technically all soldiers received pay, although hostilities, economic difficulties, and a host of other reasons often made payment irregular, and many soldiers wore money belts to protect their money from theft. The typical money belt was made of cloth and had snap compartments into which national currency or military scrip (paper money) could be placed. All such belts were purchased privately, and they can, therefore, be found in a wide variety of designs and colors. As well as money, personal keepsakes were kept there. Money belts were especially common among US, British, and German troops.

The morale of World War II soldiers was often bolstered by the availability of pictures and drawings of movie stars in pin-up poses. The 1930s drawings by American artists such as Elvgren and Moran of

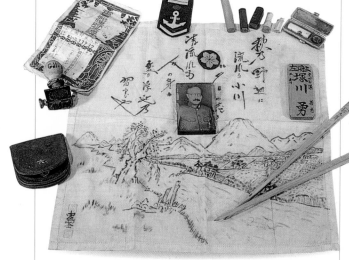

ABOVE **These Japanese personal items were collected by US Marine Corps Sergeant E. C. Anthony during the** intense fighting at Guadalcanal in February 1943.

ABOVE **All soldiers carried personal photographs with them, a practice that was not** encouraged but could not be prevented by the authorities.

PERSONAL ITEMS

ABOVE **British and US** standard-issue money belts were purchased privately, and were used to hold personal keepsakes as well as money.

ABOVE **A Japanese bamboo cup such as this would have been in everyday use.**

BELOW **German chocolate candy tin.**

LEFT **German standard-issue personal items – comb, pencil, identification papers, mask glasses, shoe laces, and 2 pfennigs – and a personal snuff box.**

Betty Grable, Rita Hayward, Jane Russell, and a host of other starlets graced the walls of barracks and wallets of the troops, and no collection of World War II memorabilia would be complete without a few examples of this art.

Superstition and warfare go together, and many soldiers, especially Americans, carried one or more good luck items. While one hears most about the proverbial rabbit's foot, the range of items used by soldiers is almost unlimited. A rifle that never jammed, or a cigarette case that stopped a bullet are the more practical examples. Whenever you acquire a World War II personal kit and cannot think of the use for one or more of the items, remember the role of the good luck token. If a collector is really lucky, he may find a cigarette pack with one cigarette turned upside down. This was the lucky cigarette, the last one to be smoked from a pack.

The carrying of personal rings and watches was discouraged. Occasionally a married soldier would carry his wedding band on his identification tag cord, and most officers wore non-military issue watches. Just before discharge, soldiers often purchased rings bearing the insignia of their branch of service or unit. These do survive and can be found by collectors.

As battles raged and goods were in short supply, stripping the equipment and personal gear from a fallen foe had more to do with survival than greed or the desire to acquire a souvenir. Foodstuffs and clothing were often taken out of necessity, but when these items were no longer needed, they were frequently retained rather than discarded.

It was a common practice to strip a fallen or captured soldier of his personal gear and items, and cigarettes, lighters, photographs, wallets, and watches were eagerly sought by the victorious soldier. Especially prized were items associated with an enemy who had fought well – an accurate sniper or an accomplished troop commander, for example.

Serious questions have been raised about the ethical aspects of collecting personal souvenirs, such as rings and watches that were acquired on the field of battle, and works of art and other treasures that were "liberated" from museums and private homes. Much of this material was returned as a result of the War Crimes Commissions of the late 1940s and early 1950s, but many items were missed.

BRITISH HEATERS

LEFT & BELOW **British heaters, which were a private purchase, and an enamel cup, which was standard issue.**

LEFT **A German leather map case.**

Each collector must live with his or her own conscience. The authors strongly recommend that every effort be made to return personal items to their rightful owners or to their heirs, even though, in the majority of cases, this will not be practicable. Nevertheless, the effort should be made: think of the anguish of families of missing in action personnel – knowing the fate of a relative even after 50 years might help to ease some of the suffering.

··· COLLECTING PERSONAL GEAR ···

Personal items fall into two main categories – those articles issued by the military and those purchased privately or received from home. Few collectors regard personal items as a principal focus for acquisition, and most collections of such articles are secondary collections, designed to complement a major collection of, say, uniforms. Remember that these are personal items. Whenever possible, try to acquire the name and a short history of the soldier who used the item.

There is, in addition, the category of official and "unofficial" souvenirs acquired by service men. Almost every Allied soldier returned home with one or more items that might be described as the "spoils of war" or as booty. In many cases these articles survived long after uniforms and other equipment had been discarded because they were the object of particular remembrances and stories.

Collectors should always understand that much of this material is sensitive and dangerous, and

ABOVE **Examples of service lighters issued to the Allied soldiers.**

discretion must always be exercised in respect of the first and care in respect of the second. However, once dealt with, these concerns should not prevent this material from being collected and displayed, for these items provide the opportunity to develop a specialized, meaningful, and personal collection. Once again, value is enhanced when the personal story is retained with the items.

PERSONAL EFFECTS

Several collectors have become fascinated by the adaptability of the combat soldier, and they collect equipment and other items that have been altered and personalized – a pair of pistol grips made from aircraft canopy Plexiglas with a picture of a favorite pin-up underneath, for example – and the late 1980s witnessed a craze for decorated World War II leather bomber jackets.

A popular souvenir in the period following World War I had been the spent artillery shell that had been decorated with punched patterns and often included the names of famous battles. The tradition continued throughout World War II, and soldiers and sailors were ingenious in their creativity. Shell casings were used to make ashtrays, lamps, matchbox covers, saki cups, salt and pepper shakers, toys (especially aircraft), and a host of other items. An excellent collection of these novelties can be assembled.

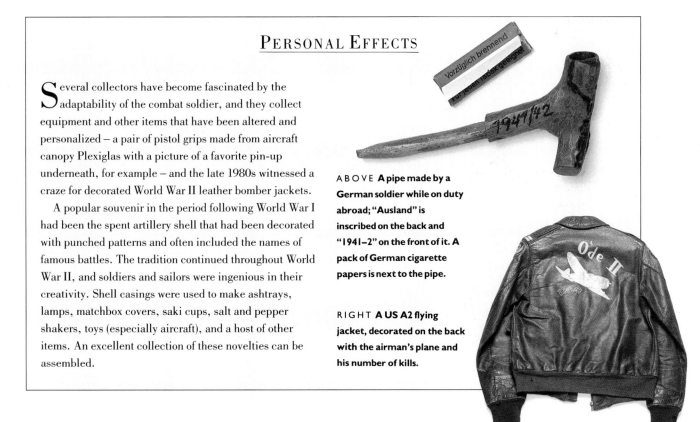

ABOVE **A pipe made by a German soldier while on duty abroad; "Ausland" is inscribed on the back and "1941-2" on the front of it. A pack of German cigarette papers is next to the pipe.**

RIGHT **A US A2 flying jacket, decorated on the back with the airman's plane and his number of kills.**

FLAGS AND BANNERS

Flags and pennons are among the more popular spoils of war, a tradition that dates back to antiquity. Military and many public museums – and even some churches – contain displays of military flags, both those of victorious units adorned with battle commendations and those of defeated units taken as trophies. Many tales of military glory revolve around an individual soldier who fought bravely and often died while protecting his nation's or his unit's flag or banner.

In the European Theater the tide of battle frequently turned during the war, and unit flags were often lost and then recaptured. US forces, for example, recovered a large number of captured British and French flags after the Italian withdrawal from North Africa. It was common practice during World War II for the soldier or soldiers who had captured a flag to sign their names on it as an indication of their victory.

In addition to unit flags, many individual soldiers carried flags. Personal Japanese flags often bore characters along the border or radiating from the central red disk. In many cases these were prayers or the names of the soldier's family and friends. Japanese soldiers carried these 18 × 24in silk flags near to their hearts.

The demand for war souvenirs in the rear encouraged the creation of fakes and forgeries, and many soldiers admitted to making counterfeit material – a Japanese flag could, for example, be made from parachute silk and iodine. Collectors should check all such items very carefully to make sure they are authentic.

ABOVE **A captured Japanese flag bearing prayers and the signatures of the** soldier's family and friends. It was traditionally carried as close to the heart as possible.

DECORATIONS

Military decorations and medals were common souvenirs. Some decorations and medals – the American Purple Heart, which was awarded to wounded soldiers, for example – were issued while the soldier was recuperating, and soldiers frequently carried them in action.

German Iron Crosses were especially prized. Among the premier examples were the Iron Cross, First Class with its screw back and case, while a Knight's Cross or the Iron Cross with case was the most highly prized of all. This was awarded posthumously to those who had shown the Reich exemplary service. Collectors should be on the alert for unidentified and unnumbered Iron Crosses, and also for the many modern reproductions that now exist.

ABOVE **German Iron Cross, First Class.**

LEFT **The Purple Heart was awarded to US soldiers wounded during combat.**

OFFICIAL SOUVENIRS

During World War II a number of non-military items were made to be sold as souvenirs to the troops. Many of these were associated with a specific military base, and they ranged from postcards to pillow covers.

Silk and fancy pillow covers were especially popular with US troops. Often rather gaudy in appearance, the covers featured a patriotic, a sentimental, or a location motif. Patriotic covers usually stressed a specific branch of service or a unit, while the most popular sentimental covers focused on mothers and sweethearts. Covers for wives and sisters are much harder to find. Most sentimental covers also contained a verse of poetry, considered corny by today's standards, but taken seriously in the early 1940s. Location pillow covers either related to a specific military base or to a large leave city such as San Francisco or Washington, D.C.

The returning soldier had only a limited opportunity to shop for something to take home to his mother, wife, or sweetheart, and one of the most popular items was the fancy, embroidered souvenir handkerchief. The theme tended to match those found on the pillow covers, although some carried martial themes, ranging from ships to branches of service. One of the most commonly found forms of decoration are flag motifs. When two flags were featured, one was generally that of a liberated country, and the second was that of the liberating armed force.

Printed textile souvenirs, although less common and less colorful than embroidered examples, were still of good quality, and collectors have learned to be suspicious of any poorly made souvenir textiles.

Jewelry was also designed to have direct appeal to the soldier, and German soldiers in occupied countries were especially eager buyers of jewelry as gifts to take or send home.

ABOVE **A matchbox showing the Manchurian Railway taken after the Japanese surrender (left); a** pair of Japanese propaganda matchboxes showing caricatures of Churchill and Roosevelt (right).

ABOVE **Dutch souvenir cards and a handkerchief celebrating the liberation of** Luxembourg by US troops. These were among the more easily acquired mementoes.

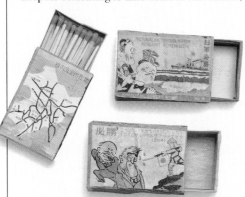

LEFT AND RIGHT **Numerous silk and fancy cushion and pillow covers were produced as official souvenirs for returning US soldiers. The range of pictorial themes and color-combinations is vast, and some collectors specialize in this one area alone.**

THE HOME FRONT

CHAPTER 5

W orld War II was fought on the home front as well as on the battlefield. Factories and farms were expected to manufacture and produce the articles required by the enormous military establishment, while the workers and their families had to make do with what was left.

Life on the home front was complex, and no aspect was untouched by the war. Civil defense, home front propaganda, and the sacrifices made for the war effort were subjects of daily conversation and action, and at the same time those who were left behind were urged to keep up the soldiers' morale by writing letters of encouragement and by sending "care" parcels.

One of the major changes to have occurred in the field of World War II collecting has been the growing recognition by collectors of the key role played by the home front and of the wealth of material that is still available. Poster collectors used to acquire examples from the 1930s and early 1940s for their visual imagery and their links with famous artists and illustrators. These collectors must now compete with people who see these posters as significant social documents in the interpretation of social and domestic life in wartime.

BELOW **A famous British poster from the "Careless Words Costs Lives" series.**

ABOVE **Two blackout lamps, the one on the right has a special revolving filter** to change the color of the light.

ABOVE **A Nazi flag, arm band, banner, mine marker, and home guard arm band. Collectors often prefer to** acquire small flags and pennants, although larger ones are much more common.

············ CIVIL DEFENSE ············

Almost the entire civilian populations of some countries were involved in civil defense. Many parts of Europe were subject to bombing raids; those that were not, feared that they might be.

In the United States civil defense was taken to extremes. Germany had no planes capable of bombing America nor aircraft carriers from which such planes could be launched. Although the Japanese were capable of landing a force on the Pacific coast, no such plans to do this were ever made. Nevertheless, even though such inland cities as Chicago had no cause to fear, it, in common with tens of thousands of cities, towns, and rural communities, regularly practiced blackouts and other defense measures. Although they had no practical purpose, such activities did serve to maintain morale and to strengthen the nation's commitment to backing the war effort.

In Britain, large parts of which were nightly subjected to sustained and indiscriminate bombing, civil defense played a large part in the lives of everyone. Civil defense personnel, both men and women, wore blue wool uniforms with buttons bearing a crown and the letters CD. They were issued with special helmets – the standard-issue British Mk1 helmet – which was painted a dark color with the initials CD in white, and with special gas masks. There was work for anyone who volunteered, and units included firemen, bomb disposal officers, and air raid wardens. Large numbers of the special gas masks were issued, and many have survived and are available to collectors.

The blackout is one of the most frequently remembered civilian experiences of World War II, and every country sold blackout kits for every possible eventuality, from automobile headlights to home windows. When an air raid warning occurred, people were required to make their home or work place pitch black so that it was not visible from the air, and local wardens patrolled the streets to see that this goal was accomplished. In Britain the blackout was observed even when no warning was sounded.

CIVIL DEFENSE

ABOVE **A British woman's civil defense jacket. The buttons on such jackets always bore the initials CD, even though the materials used changed during the course of the war from metal to plastic.**

BELOW **A civilian sign at an air raid shelter; an air raid warden's whistle; a warden's badge; and house plaque.**

H.M.O.W.

DURING AIR RAID CONDITIONS THIS REFUGE IS DESIGNED TO HOUSE ○ ○ PERSONS WITH AN ADEQUATE AIR SUPPLY. EXERTION SHOULD BE AVOIDED. SMOKING IS STRICTLY PROHIBITED

A.R.P.

WARDEN CITY OF WESTMINSTER

An often overlooked group of collectibles from Britain is the material relating to the Home Guard, which served as a security force and was especially active in capturing enemy fliers whose aircraft had been shot down. The Home Guard's uniform and equipment were superficially like those of the combat troops, but close inspection will quickly reveal the differences. At the beginning of the war it was not uncommon to find Home Guard troops in civilian dress; as the war drew to a close their uniforms closely resembled those of British regulars, although there were major differences in accessories such as ammunition pouches. Members of the Home Guard were often equipped with US weapons obtained under the terms of the Lend-Lease scheme.

Other countries followed the British example in developing civil defense units and some form of home guard – for example, beach watchers and airplane spotters were appointed in the United States. Uniforms, helmets, and a wealth of literature supported these efforts.

When you are collecting material associated with the public service wartime personnel, both paid and volunteer, do not overlook the established civilian sectors such as the police, ambulance men and women, and fire fighters, all of whom made major contributions to the home front.

The International Red Cross was the primary agency through which individual donations were funneled to the troops, and its personnel served on every home and war front. Red Cross uniforms, insignia, equipment, and literature have already attracted the attention of World War II collectors, and premium prices are paid for some items. The Red Cross was also responsible for transporting parcels intended for Allied prisoners of war and for supervising the camps in which Axis prisoners were held.

The British Red Cross was extremely active, organizing first aid courses for civil defense personnel and the civilian population in general, and establishing emergency aid stations to feed and house victims of the bombing. In the United States the Red Cross served as the intermediary between families and the military, notifying soldiers serving overseas of births and deaths of relatives. Like their British counterparts, US Red Cross personnel continually tried to gain access to POW camps to carry out inspections. The German Red Cross was organized along military lines, and the uniforms were similar to the standard army issue. A highly collectible item is the dagger that was carried by German Red Cross officers and enlisted personnel.

···· WAR BONDS AND DONATIONS ····

Many countries helped to finance the war through the sale of saving and war bonds, and in order to encourage sales, war bond stamps were often sold for just a few cents so that they could be purchased as and when funds allowed, pasted in a book, and redeemed for a bond once the book was filled. Many personalities from the movies, radio, and the stage were enlisted to help with the promotion and sale of war bonds, and some collectors specialize in this one aspect of the war on the home front.

Often war bond drives were linked with donation drives. In 1942, for example, the German bond drive for soldiers on the Eastern Front also requested the donation of winter clothing, including furs. Individuals at home were encouraged to make items for use by the troops in the field. Women knitted and knitted and knitted, and out flowed a wide variety of balaclavas, comforters, scarves, socks, sweaters, vests, wristlets, and watch caps. This aspect of the war has not attracted the attention of collectors, and there is an opportunity to assemble a specialized but highly personal and worthwhile collection of instructions and end products.

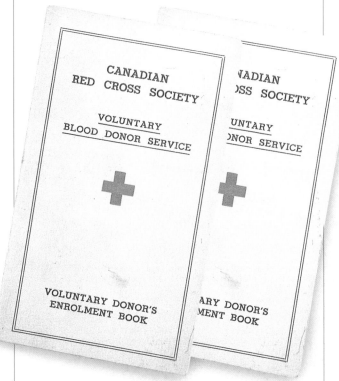

ABOVE **The registration book of a Canadian volunteer** blood donor was used to check individual donations.

ABOVE **A US Red Cross worker's musette bag. These small bags, which were made** of canvas or leather, were used for carrying toilet articles and so on.

PAPER MONEY

National and military scrip (paper money) was a popular souvenir, and soldiers collected various denominations and colors. In some cases, occupying forces simply printed or stamped existing scrip with their own identification marks and this too, can be collected.

LEFT **Occupation scrip from France and Germany. Scrip like this was also issued in Italy and Japan.**

ABOVE **Foreign scrip was a popular souvenir. This Dutch money was issued during the German occupation.**

PROPAGANDA MATERIAL

War propaganda was everywhere – cigarette and gum cards, displays of captured war equipment, pins focusing on national and military heroes, matchbox covers, movies, music, novels, posters, and of course, on the radio. The key is to collect by type – posters, for example – or theme – patriotic, character assassination, industrial production effort and so on.

One of the most important propaganda vehicles was the postal service, and both the Americans and Germans were particularly adept at using the mail for propaganda purposes. Letterheads, envelopes, postcards, stamps, and even the cancellation stamps helped to convey a wartime message. German stamps were especially noted for their martial and patriotic themes, while many American letters were canceled with a V for victory.

RIGHT **War issue theme playing cards: (left to right) Australian Comfort Fund,** **"Bulldog" Churchill and two sets of Free French cards.**

····· LETTERS AND POSTCARDS ·····

Collectors have always sought war-time correspondence, especially letters written by combat soldiers and containing detailed descriptions of battles. Although letters that comment on day-to-day life are interesting, they are not particularly valuable. Especially prized are envelopes featuring hand-drawn artwork, and examples are far more common among Axis mail than among Allied mail.

One item that has recently attracted the attention of collectors is the American V-mail system, by which letters were copied at a reduced size so that more items of mail could be sent in one bag, thus conserving space and often leading to faster delivery. As with most countries, the US postal authorities gave the highest priority to mail for the armed forces, fully realizing the value of a letter from home to the troops.

A collection of postcards can provide a visual means of documenting the war. German postcards often featured full color military artwork as a means of encouraging patriotism, and Germany was the first country to produce full color postcards depicting armed forces personnel in action.

American postcards, with their strong emphasis on humor, contrast sharply with the serious subjects of most German postcards, and several series were issued, illustrating military life in a humorous way. Postcards of military training tended to show barracks, mess hall, church, common equipment, or training exercises.

BELOW **These folding postcards were sold to soldiers to send home to their families.**

···········INTERNMENT CAMPS···········

The Allies and Axis countries maintained prisoner of war camps in their home territories as well as in occupied lands, and collectors have only recently begun to seek POW uniforms, many of which consisted of obsolete military-issue uniforms. German POWs interned in the United States wore old uniforms with the large letters PW painted on them for high visibility and to aid in their detection and capture should they escape. Two specialized areas for collectors include objects used in successful and unsuccessful escape attempts and objects delivered to prisoners in Red Cross packages.

Prisoners of war frequently passed their time by making small trinkets and other items. Among the articles that have been found are aluminum rings bearing the names and location of prisoners, sandals, and wallets. The shortages in POW camps and the failure of Red Cross parcels to arrive on a regular basis forced prisoners to modify their uniforms for prison use, and prisoners often used the leather or fabric for craft purposes.

Collecting military POW material is an established tradition – material from British and other prison ships during the Napoleonic Wars appears on the market on a regular basis – but little is written or spoken about more recent items, largely because of their sensitive nature.

BELOW **Leather sandals, a wallet, a bag, and a ring** carved from an antler – all made by a German prisoner of war. Such objects were not made purely for use, but also to help keep the prisoner occupied.

·········FOOD AND RATIONING·········

Every country had to introduce some form of rationing during the war, and ration books, stamps, and certificates have survived in large numbers. Items such as the automobile windshield gasoline ration stickers and the red cardboard tokens used in the United States as a form of rationing currency, are hard to find. The way in which they were used made their survival unlikely.

Food was in short supply throughout much of the war. Industrial production was turned over to preparing foodstuffs for the armed forces, and civilians were encouraged to meet their own needs. In Britain and the United States Victory Garden projects were introduced, and most other countries launched similar schemes. Items ranging from posters to seed packets were produced in support of these projects.

Recycling was a vital contribution to the home front, and even foodstuffs, such as fat and grease, were recycled. Nationwide drives were launched for aluminum, brass, steel, and other metals, and many historic decorative accessories, toys, and collectibles were lost to the war effort. The Germans recycled aircraft that had been shot down in order to recover the aluminum. The literature relating to these scrap drives, especially the posters that were produced, can serve as the basis of a specialized collection.

BELOW **The cover for a US ration book. This was intended to protect the all-** important booklets that contained the ration stamps.

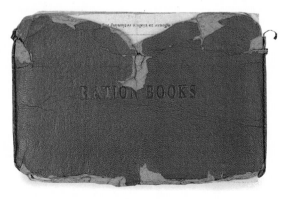

RATION BOOKS

Ration books were used to enable governments to control the allocation of resources and to ensure that scarce materials were devoted to the war effort.

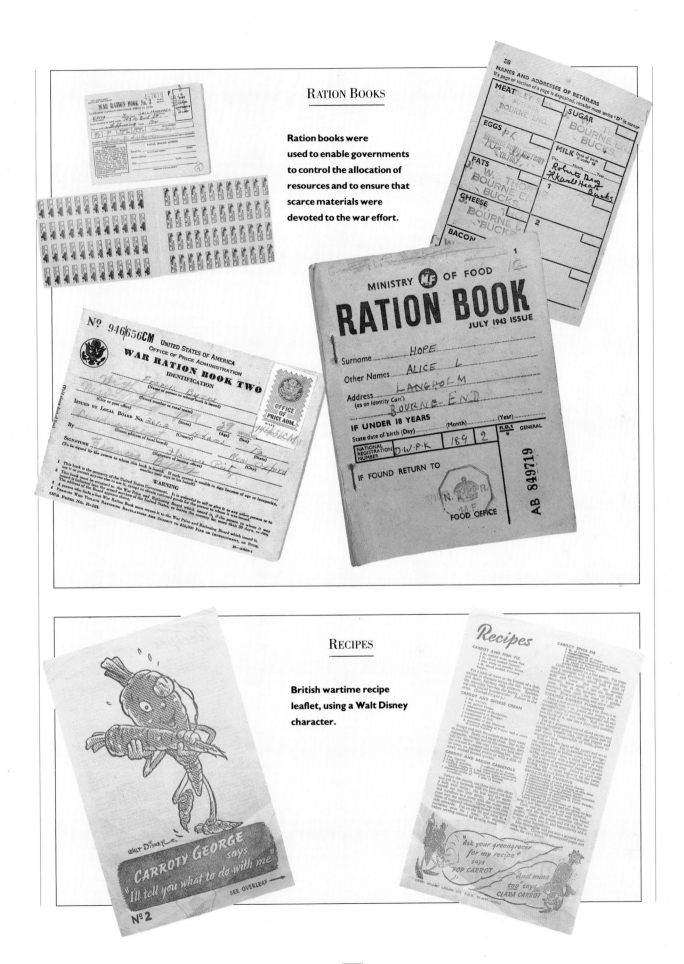

RECIPES

British wartime recipe leaflet, using a Walt Disney character.

ABOVE **Another British poster in the "Careless Talk Costs Lives" series.**

MISCELLANEOUS ITEMS

All countries issued banners, plaques, decorations, medals, and rewards to boost civilian morale and to honor the sacrifices that were made. Germany issued a Mother's Cross in three different grades, and a small pension was attached to the award. The decoration was designed not only to honor mothers with sons and daughters in military service but also to encourage women to bear children. In the United States families whose members were serving in the military would hang a banner in the window with a star or stars to indicate the number of individuals in the family who were in the service.

Although it is a rather morbid subject, some collectors specialize in the documents and other artifacts associated with the notification of death. In the United States the news often arrived by Western Union telegram; in Britain the news was delivered in person by one or more military personnel whenever possible, although when all else failed, telegrams or letters were used. Like the British, the Germans tried to deliver the dread news personally, and the principal means was a local representative of the armed forces. As the war progressed and the number of dead increased, the principal means of notification was a letter from the unit commander. Many such letters had to be sent after long campaigns as officers reported losses they had been unable to notify immediately.

Although every nation's industry was placed on a war footing, little material has survived from the industrial effort. Some industries may still have World War II production records stuck away in a warehouse or filing cabinet in the basement – a small bicycle manufacturer during peace time might well have made parts for the Sten gun during the war, for example – yet, despite the scarcity and intrinsic interest of this material, it commands little value among collectors.

Much more eagerly sought is material relating to transportation during the war, and of this material the prime object is, of course, the poster. Look out for posters that urge civilians to limit their own travel to make more room available for troops and for examples that provide reminders not to talk about the movement of troops and supplies – "Loose lips sink ships" and "Careless talk costs lives."

Sacrifice was required of all ages. Children wore hand-me-downs and played with the toys of their older brothers and sisters who were now fighting at the front. New clothing, if it was available, was practical and often lacked style. Toys and games were developed with patriotic, upbeat, often martial themes, and children were encouraged to play soldiers.

COLLECTING FROM THE HOME FRONT

Collectors are paying more and more attention to this important area, and although home front collectibles will never surpass military items in popularity, they will no longer be relegated to the background.

Home front collectibles offer tremendous opportunities for specialization. A collection of World War II patriotic and battle-scene jigsaw puzzles would include more than 300 items if one example of every known kind were acquired. At the moment, too, with the exception of long-established

MAGAZINES

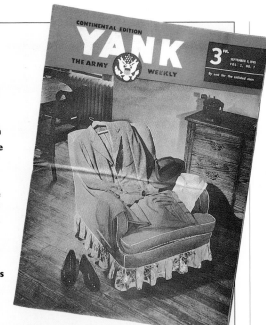

LEFT *Life* magazine was regarded by Americans as the prime source of in- depth information about the course of the war.

RIGHT *Yank*, the magazine for Allied troops, is an example of the kind of journalism that was written specifically to promote a positive view of the war. This issue is dated September 1945.

LEFT *Signal*, a German propaganda publication.

BELOW The German magazine, *Der Alder*, in its German and French editions.

collectible categories such as posters, most home front collectibles are not very expensive. A substantial collection of military-related postcards or magazines issued between 1939 and 1945 could be assembled without spending more than a few dollars for the common issues and 10 dollars for the harder to find examples.

If this is an area that interests you, resist the temptation to invest too much time and money building up a collection. At present the generation that grew up during and immediately after the war is buying this material, principally from nostalgia. Only when this generation dies will the true test of the marketability of these items occur.

KEYS TO COLLECTING

CHAPTER 6

I f you are considering collecting World War II memorabilia and articles, now is the time to begin.

Plenty of material is available, and much of it is very affordable. The fiftieth anniversary celebrations that began in 1989 have been responsible for a wealth of new material appearing on the market. In addition, soldiers who actually served in the conflict are now nearing or are past retirement age, and they are more likely to be thinking about selling any items or mementoes they have than to be wanting to acquire new articles. Collectors who are willing to make the effort have a unique opportunity to obtain items from the original owners, thus allowing them to record and preserve the stories associated with the objects they acquire.

ABOVE **A kit for testing the presence of mustard gas issued in Britain at the beginning of the war but never actually used.**

ABOVE **An embroidered armband for a member of the Military Police. These were** **often worked by hand for senior officials.**

BELOW **The joy stick weapons handle from a Messerschmitt Bf 109 and a Bf 109 chronometer. These were removed from the Messerschmitt by its pilot (ace Luftwaffe pilot, Lieutenant Helmut Macher), after the plane was severely damaged in operations over the Eastern Front.**

A key factor in determining price is, of course, the number of examples of a particular article that has actually survived. Anniversaries and high prices often have the effect of bringing hitherto hidden or forgotten items out of attics, basements, closets, and storage chests, and it takes only a few such objects to depress a market based on scarcity.

Some categories are expensive – the uniforms, small arms, and other material associated with the German and Japanese armies have long been highly sought after – but this is such a huge field that newcomers to the subject will be able to find an area that interests them and that they can afford. The field is so wide that some kind of specialization is essential.

When you are trying to select an area you should bear in mind not only your own budget, but also such practical considerations as the space that you can make available for your collection and the accessibility of the items that interest you. Although it is perfectly possible to assemble collections by mail order, most World War II items are collected by visiting stores, shops, and shows, where you can have an opportunity to inspect the items before buying them on the spot.

Before you buy anything, however, spend as much time as you can looking at collections and exhibitions. Visit military and local museums that have strong collections of militaria. Your local historical society might also have a collection of World War II items, and your local library should be able to suggest collections that are within a day's trip from your home.

These preliminary visits to museums will serve two functions. First, they will give you some idea of the range of material that is available and will give you an opportunity to decide what you find particularly interesting and, conversely but just as important, those items that you do not like and that do not interest you. Second, the visits will tell you what items museum curators think are important and worth collecting. Private collectors tend to concentrate on objects not found in museums as this gives them a greater sense of participating in the process of preserving history.

While you are making these visits to museums and collections, you should also begin to visit the special antiques and collectibles shows at which military material is sold.

The old adages "it pays to look" and "let the buyer beware" apply here. Remember that almost all the material you are going to purchase was mass-produced, often in extremely large quantities, and as you examine similar pieces, compare their condition. Discipline yourself right from the start only to buy objects that are in good or excellent condition.

At this stage you should be beginning to narrow down the categories that interest you. Compare the availability and prices of the items that you see, and begin to look out for dealers who specialize in the areas that interest you, taking the opportunity to

ABOVE **The guide Back to Civil Life was issued to Canadian troops prior to** demobilization to ease their re-entry to civilian life.

make some initial contacts. Do not make any definite decisions on the basis of only one show, however. Try to attend at least a dozen shows in different parts of the country before you make any purchases.

Take every opportunity to compare prices. There are no fixed prices for antiques and collectibles – they are worth only what someone is prepared to pay. Collectors who are just beginning to build up a collection often pay too much for common objects because they lack experience in assessing scarcity and condition. Avoid making this mistake by putting off making your first purchase until you are certain that you have looked at and compared the prices and condition of several similar articles.

It is wise to establish a budget for yourself in the early days and to stick to it. Collecting is no fun if you spend all your money quickly.

Most shows and exhibitions of militaria will include one or more dealers who sell books on collecting military items. Before you buy your first object, buy one or more of the books on the subject, especially those that relate directly to the areas of

your own interest. While you are at the show, look out for copies of the specialist newspapers and magazines that are published for enthusiasts, and use these to obtain the names and addresses of dealers who sell by mail order and of the leading military auctions. Once you start collecting seriously you will find that you buy the bulk of your objects privately through the mail or at auction.

The most obvious place to find World War II collectibles is at specialized military and gun shows. These shows occur on a regular basis and follow an established circuit, and once you have attended one show, you will have no trouble in finding another. Almost all of them feature a table loaded with announcements of forthcoming events.

General antiques and collectibles shows are now good places to find World War II items, which quickly find their way into the military and gun markets. As you collect, you will hear numerous stories about how a particular collector went to a local antiques show and bought an extremely scarce item at an incredibly low price because the general antiques dealer did not know what they had. The question you should ask is how much time did the

BELOW **Luminous buttons and arm band for use in Britain during blackouts and a set of blackout curtain fasteners to ensure absolutely no light escaped.**

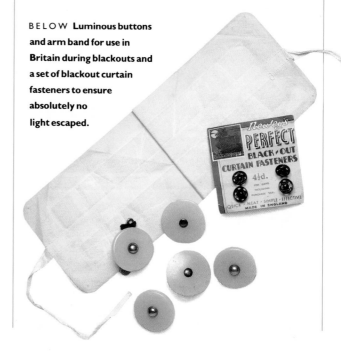

ABOVE **Safe conduct passes, issued by Allied Expeditionary Force members to any** **surrendering army personnel. These were usually distributed by air drop.**

collector waste in pursuit of this single find. Shows devoted exclusively to paper ephemera are the exception to the rule, for they often contain a wealth of World War II items.

The sale of war-related material has long been the province of the specialized dealer. The larger dealers publish sale catalogs once a year or sometimes more often, and although you will usually have to pay to obtain copies, this will be money well

BELOW **A poster issued after V-E Day reminding** **Great Britain that Japan was, as yet, undefeated.**

spent. Back issues of these catalogs will provide important information about prices.

Within the past decade there has been a small but steady growth in military mail auctions. Instead of offering material for direct sale, some dealers prepare catalogs for distribution to potential buyers, and they then take bids over the telephone. Occasionally regular one-day auctions are held, but these are not common.

Small arms are regularly sold at auction, and established collectors know that these auctions are worth attending because they often contain supporting military uniforms, equipment, and personal gear, which tend to be of little interest to specialist gun collectors. Opportunities for bargain purchases abound.

Although open market sales of World War II collectibles take place on a regular basis, a surprisingly large amount of goods changes hands privately. It is important, therefore, to make contact with other collectors as quickly as possible. Your first step is to join a collectors' club and to attend the regional and national meetings of the organization. Military collectors can sometimes be difficult and secretive – established collectors are reluctant to reveal their sources; some never will. Do not become discouraged. One of the keys to joining the inner circle of collectors is persistence.

Every collector dreams of buying at source, and this is still possible for collectors of World War II material. Begin with your own relatives and friends, asking them if they know people who participated in the war. Visit them and ask if they have any war-related material that they would be willing to sell. Do not expect your success rate to be high – you will fail in your efforts more frequently than you will succeed. Nevertheless, there will be times you are successful, and you should persevere.

Your search is likely to be fraught with danger, the major pitfalls being reproductions, copycats, conversions and fakes. Keeping the following points in the back of your mind will help you avoid some costly mistakes:

● Large numbers of reproduction uniforms, weapons and equipment are made for World War II re-enactment purposes. Since the goal is authenticity, many of these pieces are marked in the same way as period pieces. Your own researches and trustworthy dealers are the keys to identifying this material.

● Beware of items that are similar to military issue but that were produced for the civilian market. Camping equipment such as mess kits and canteens are examples of this.

● Military equipment evolves continually. Forces of occupation and forces that fought in Korea in the 1950s used equipment that is often similar to World War II equipment. However, much of this equipment was made to later models that were not issued during World War II. It is important to learn to distinguish between the different models.

● Many World War II paper items – posters, for example – have been reprinted. Look out for variations in size, colour tones and quality of paper.

Collectors often feel most comfortable when they are collecting what they know, and many World War II collectibles tend to have an air of familiarity and similarity about them. Do not be afraid to explore new ground. Two sub-categories that appear to offer real collecting potential, even though they occurred after the end of the war, are occupation zone collectibles and Cold War collectibles. It would be a mistake to assume that the war ended in 1945 – the fighting may have ended in that year, but the consequences continued for decades.

Finally, remember that any collection of objects is nothing more than an assembly of inanimate items, each of which stands and falls on its own merits. This rather depersonalized approach, especially as it relates to World War II collectibles, overlooks the fact that wars are fought by human beings. War affects a much wider area than the battlefield, and the lives of large numbers of civilians and non-combatants are significantly altered. It is essential that this human side of warfare is not lost when you assemble your collection. Always make sure that you preserve the human element in any collection that you acquire.

BELOW **A poster showing how those at home were not forgotten.**

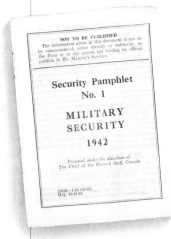
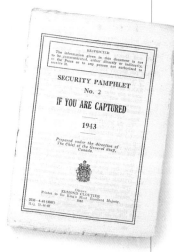

ABOVE **Canadian military intelligence security pamphlets from 1942–3. Items like this are rare –** **most were destroyed to prevent any likelihood of organisational compromise.**

········ COLLECTORS' CLUBS ·········

AMERICAN SOCIETY OF MILITARY INSIGNIA COLLECTORS

526 Lafayette Avenue, Palmerton, PA 18071

ASSOCIATION OF AMERICAN MILITARY UNIFORM COLLECTORS

PO Box 1876, Elyria, OH 44036

COMPANY OF MILITARY HISTORIANS

North Main Street, Westbrook, CT 06498

IMPERIAL GERMAN MILITARY COLLECTORS' ASSOCIATION

82 Atlantic St., Keyport, NJ 07735

MILITARY VEHICLE COLLECTORS' CLUB

PO Box 1748, Union, NJ 07083

NATIONAL WORLD WAR II HISTORICAL PRESERVATION FOUNDATION

2812 Jermantown Road, Oakton, VA 22124

ORDERS AND MEDALS SOCIETY OF AMERICA

PO Box 484, Glassboro, NJ 08028

SHARKHUNTERS

PO Box 1539, Hernando, FL 32642

WESTERN FRONT ASSOCIATION

743 11th Avenue, Huntingdon, WV 25701

················ MUSEUMS ·················

The following are only a selection of the many museums devoted to military history with displays dealing with World War II.

NATIONAL ARMED FORCES HISTORICAL MUSEUM

Smithsonian Institute, Washington DC 20560

UNITED STATES MARINE CORPS MUSEUM

Marine Corps School, Quantico, Virginia

WAR MEMORIAL MUSEUM OF VIRGINIA

9285 Warwick Road, Huntingdon Park, Newport News, Virginia

WEST POINT MUSEUM

United States Military Academy, West Point, New York

············· BIBLIOGRAPHY ··············

BARNES, G. M. *Weapons of World War II*. New York: D. Van Nostrand Company, Inc.: 1947

BAUR, EDDY. *Illustrated WW II Encyclopedia*. Jaspard Polus Monaco: H. S. Stuttman, Inc.: 1978

CARTER, J. ANTHONY. *Allied Bayonets of World War II*. New York: Arco Publishing Co: 1969

DAVIS, BRIAN L. *German Army Uniforms and Insignia, 1933–45*. New York: The World Publishing Co.: 1972

DILLY, ROY. *Japanese Army Uniforms and Equipment, 1939–1945*. London: Almark Publishing Co.: 1970

FISCH, ROBERT. *Field Equipment of the Infantry, 1914–1945*. Sykesville, MD: Greenburg Publishing: 1989

FLAYDERMAN, NORMAN. *Flayderman's Guide to Antique American Firearms and Their Values, Fifth Edition*. Northbrook, IL: DBI Books: 1990

HOGG, IAN V., AND JOHN WEEKS. *Military Small Arms of the 20th Century*. Secaucus, NJ: Chartwell Books: 1990

KATHER, PHILIP. *The U.S. Army 1941–1945*. London: Osprey Publications: 1984

MOLLO, ANDREW. *Army Uniforms of World War Two*. London: Blandford Press: 1973

ROBLES, PHILIP K. *United States Military Medals and Ribbons*. Rutland, VT: Charles E. Tuttle Co.: 1971

SCHICK, L. T. *Battledress*. Boston, MA: Little, Brown & Company: 1978

SILVIA, STEPHEN W., AND MICHAEL J. O'DONNEL. *Uniforms, Weapons, and Equipment 1939–1945 WWII G.I.* Orange, VA: Moss Publications: 1982

TAYLOR, HUGH PAGE, AND JAMES R. BENDER. *Uniforms, Organization and History of the Waffen SS*. Palo Alto, CA: D. D. Assoc.: 1969

VERNON, SYDNEY B. *Vernon's Collectors' Guide to Orders, Medals, and Decorations (with Valuations)*. Published by author: 1986

Handbook on the British Army with Supplements on the Royal Air Force and Civilian Defense Organizations TM 30–410. Washington, D.C.: United States War Department: 1942

Handbook on German Military Forces TM-E 451. Washington, D.C.: United States War Department: March 15, 1945

Handbook on the Italian Military Forces TM 30–420. Washington D.C.: United States War Department: 1943

Handbook on Japanese Military Forces TM-E-30-480. Washington, D.C.: United States War Department: October 1, 1944

INDEX

1942

MONTH	WESTERN FRONT	EASTERN FRONT	MEDITERRANEAN	PACIFIC
June	1: Allied air raids on Essen and the Ruhr begin	26: German victory at Kharkov	1: British 150th Brigade defeated by Rommel 15: Battle of Pantelleria 26: Axis troops enter Mersa Matruh	4-7: Battle of Midway 27: MacArthur reveals plans for the recapture of New Britain, New Ireland, and Admiralty Islands
July		12: Russians establish Stalingrad front		
August			8: Eisenhower appointed commander of Operation Torch 10: Start of Operation Pedestal to relieve Malta	
September		33: Battle for Stalingrad begins		
October			23: Second Battle of El Alamein begins	26: Battle of Santa Cruz
November	11: Germany invades unoccupied France		16: Tunisia in Axis hands	12-13: Battle of Guadalcanal

1943

MONTH	WESTERN FRONT	EASTERN FRONT	MEDITERRANEAN	PACIFIC
January			14: Casablanca Conference opens	
February		2: Germany resistance at Stalingrad ends		
March				3-5: Battle of the Bismarck Sea 12-15: Pacific Military Conference held in Washington
April		19: Massacre of Jews in Warsaw ghetto		
May	27: Allies drop 1,000 tons of bombs on Essen		12: General von Arnim surrenders to Allies in Tunisia	
June				30: Operation Cartwheel begins
July			10: Operation Husky begins 25: Mussolini jailed	
August			17: Patton's troops enter Sicily	
September			10: Germans occupy Rome	
October			13: Italy declares war on Germany	
November		11: Kiev retaken		20: Operation Galvanic begins 28: Roosevelt, Churchill and Stalin meet at Teheran
December			7: Eisenhower appointed C-in-C of Operation Overlord	

1944

MONTH	WESTERN FRONT	EASTERN FRONT	MEDITERRANEAN	PACIFIC
January		27: Leningrad blockade lifted		31: Invasion of Marshall Islands begins
February			15: Bombing of Monte Cassino begins	